10/93

Albuque
6400
Albu
D0484989

REFLECTIONS OF A ROCK LOBSTER

Rock Lobster *n.* **1.** a crustacean having a firm shell for defense against predators, but lacking claws. **2.** a song popular with young people in the early nineteen-eighties.

Reflections of a Rock Lobster

a story about growing up gay

by Aaron Fricke

Alyson Publications, Inc. • **Boston**

Copyright ©1981 by Aaron Fricke
All rights reserved. Typeset and printed in the United States
  of America.

First published in 1981 by ALYSON PUBLICATIONS, INC.
as a paperback original.

10 9 8 7 6 5

Library of Congress
Catalog Card No.: 81-65806
    Fricke, Aaron
        Reflections of a Rock Lobster:
        A Story about Growing Up Gay
    Boston, Mass.   Alyson Publications

ISBN 0 932870 09 0

The names of some students and other characters in this story have
been changed.

To my beloved Hedy Lamarr,

        and Judge Pettine
            Jim Barry
            John Gaffney
            Lynette Labinger
            Chuck Noice
            John Ward

        and Sasha Alyson
            without whom I would never
            have had the opportunity
            to write this book.

721
FRICKE

Contents

Preface

This is a book about growing up gay. But before I get into the story, I want to briefly discuss the questions that so many people have asked me. The most common is: "Why are you gay?"

The popular belief is that homosexuality is caused by a domineering mother. My mother and father both gave me a great deal of love and attention; by no means was my mother emotionally domineering. And at 4'7" my mother is certainly not physically domineering either.

Another theory is that a sexual assault by an older man leads boys to become homosexual. I was never sexually assaulted during my childhood. There was the time when I was seven and my sixteen-year-old babysitter tried to make me touch her rear end — but I merely passed the incident off as straight whimsiness and made her give me ten dollars not to tell my parents. I don't see how this could have made me switch sexual preferences.

So I did not have a domineering mother, my parents loved me, and I was never sexually assaulted by an older person. Furthermore, my mother was not doing speed at the time of conception, I was never exposed to high level radiation, and I never read a Truman Capote book before age ten. Why, then, am I gay?

I think we are on the wrong track to spend too much time on this question. A more important question is: Why do so many people fear anyone who is different from them and thus label them sick or evil? But people never ask that. Instead they ask: "Then why *did* you choose homosexuality?" *I* didn't choose homosexuality: homosexuality chose me. People do not wake up in the morning and say, "Gee, I think I'll be a homosexual." The only choice I had was whether to nurture or stifle my homosexual feelings. I merely chose not to be forced into "acceptable" social conduct.

Often people tell me homosexuality is wrong because it does not occur in nature: "It is not natural." In fact, homosexuality has been observed in many animals in the wild. But even so, human beings do many things that are unique to our species. Does that make these traits unnatural? Only humans play tennis; does this make those of us who have the desire to play tennis "unnatural"?

People also ask, "What is it that you hate about yourself that made you become a homosexual?" What a ridiculous question! I never had a low self-esteem that would make me gay. At one point, though, the reverse happened. Being homosexual led me to have a low self-esteem when I first became aware of society's attitudes about homosexuality.

In short, it is as impossible to explain why homosexuality exists as to explain why heterosexuality exists. Natural events rarely have one identifiable cause. How do you answer a question like, "Why does a stream flow?" There are so many possible answers. A poet, a scientist, a cardio-vascular nurse would each give a different reason. And maybe none would be correct. We must accept the simple fact that streams do flow. Homosexuality *does* exist. And now, let's get on with the story.

Here I am at age three, with Santa.

Childhood

Cumberland, Rhode Island, is a small, sparsely populated town twenty miles north of Providence. Cumberland grew up around the textile factories that flourished during the late 1800's and early 1900's. Some of those textile mills are still in business, but most of Cumberland's population today consists of middle-class workers and their families, who have defected from urban blight.

Cumberland is a pretty town, with all the appeal of a typical New England setting. The mills are at one end, out of the way, and an occasional farm keeps the town from feeling too urban. Most of the people are Roman Catholic.

In 1964, when I was two years old, my family moved from Providence to Cumberland. I think this move to a new city was a cutting of apron strings for them. It removed the constraints of family and tradition and gave my parents a freedom to live as they chose in the somewhat pioneer atmosphere of Cumberland. Any possible vision of the future could be fulfilled in this escape villa. It was a town where white collar workers could live their lives and raise their children as they chose, with no surprises.

Well, almost none. Cumberland, Rhode Island, is where I grew up gay.

In my early childhood Cumberland was a wonderful place to live. I spent many memorable years in the two-story white house my parents bought. It was on a dead end street at the top of a hill in North Cumberland, with a beautiful view of the neighboring town of Lincoln.

My father worked as an independent ships' pilot out of the port of Providence. His seagoing career made it impossible for him to be present all the time during my childhood. There were no nine-to-five hours for Dad. He could be called out at five o'clock in the morning and spend days piloting a single ship from the port of Providence to New York or New London. But he didn't let his unconventional schedule infringe on our relationship. We spent much time together simply because he wanted to make that time for me.

My mother never worked outside the home after she married. She spent most of her time taking care of me and my sister Cheryl. Mom did a very good job, and I developed a deep love for my mother and for my father.

Cheryl was born eight years before me. Because of our great age difference, my sister and I were not particularly close during childhood. In my eyes she was another adult, almost a third parent, and I looked up to her. Yet my parents reprimanded her as they did me, so I knew she was really closer to my status level.

One day when I was about six, while watching a Batman episode with Cheryl, I casually commented on the anatomical proportions of Batman. I knew no reason to stifle my aroused sexual feelings, so I just mentioned that I liked what

I saw. Cheryl freaked out. It was my first lesson that talking about this subject made people upset.

This was the first time I had spoken of my sexual thoughts although I had been having those thoughts for as long as I could remember. Already I was undressing my GI Joe dolls, and I had messed around with some of my male playmates, but it never crossed my mind to mention my feelings to anyone. After the Batman incident, I never expressed my sexual observations to my sister again. But beyond that, this incident had no major effect on me. I still had no idea that my sexuality was considered "wrong."

My sexual exploits with my neighborhood playmates continued. I lived a busy homosexual childhood, somehow managing to avoid venereal disease through all my toddler years. By first grade I was sexually active with many friends. In fact, a small group of us regularly met in the grammar school lavatory to perform fellatio on one another. A typical week's schedule would be Aaron and Michael on Monday during lunch; Michael and Johnny on Tuesday after school; Fred and Timmy at noon Wednesday; Aaron and Timmy after school on Thursday. None of us ever got caught, but we never worried about it anyway. We all understood that what we were doing was not to be discussed freely with adults but we viewed it as a fun sort of confidential activity. None of us had any guilty feelings about it; we figured everyone did it. Why shouldn't they?

One friend I was very close to was Billy Marlen. Billy was a year behind me in school yet we got along well together. In our friendship, a special camaraderie existed that was rare in my other friendships. There was a brotherhood that does not often occur even between brothers. We shared our toys and spent many summer days building sandcastles on the beach. On rainy days I'd walk down to Billy's house where we spent the day reading books and building racetracks and playing sex therapist in his basement. We were human beings who knew no social inhibitions and were willing to explore our sexuality to its fullest.

We found vestibules around his house and mine where we could hide on rainy days while our mothers prepared a hot lunch. One day, Billy's mother discovered us in a closet. It had a long passageway leading to a secluded space in the back so she saw nothing of what had transpired a few minutes earlier. Yet, when she heard our shuffling about in the dark it lead her to holler in a quivering voice, *"Aaron! Billy! Get out of the closet. Now!"*

She seemed overwhelmed, as upset as my sister had been during the Batman incident. It was only a little unsettling for me; just another lesson that there were many feelings I could not share with adults.

Billy and I maintained our friendship and became very close during second grade. Love was an integral part of our relationship — and a nice relationship it was. We went to the movies together; our parents took us on vacations and to amusement parks together; we even went trick-or-treating together on Halloween.

On Halloween of 1971, I was in fourth grade and Billy was in third. He dressed as a lumberjack and I went in drag as his damsel. Our parents let us go through the neighborhood; they probably wouldn't have if they had known what we would stumble upon.

Billy and I had been running from one house to another in Gadoury Plat for a while when we came upon a small house surrounded by a white picket fence. Going up the front walk we heard music and laughter inside. Somebody was having a party. We rang the doorbell.

A person wearing a long flowery gown, high heels, nylons, ball earrings and a blond wig answered the door. Certain masculine features made it obvious that he was not a woman.

We said the customary "Trick or Treat!"

"Well, well, well, it's Darling Daisy Dumpling and her him. What are your names?" he asked. When we told him he exclaimed. . . .

"Purple passion in my ovaries!" realizing that I was a boy.

"Trick or Treat!" Billy and I repeated in unison.

"No comment," said the man, dropping candy into our plastic pumpkins. "Now girls, it's not unobvious that you got a bit o' Jane in you. Well, don't you fight it honey."

"OK," we said, totally unaware of what he was referring to. Billy and I then scampered off along the pathway of the house.

Billy and I had many good times together during the year, but he moved from Cumberland in January and I lost a close friend.

Sex continued for me but it was not the same as it was with Billy. It was always readily available after school, during school, at cub scouts, at Sunday School or at summer camp, but that certain element that Billy added was gone.

In fourth grade, I had my first confrontation with the Cumberland school system. For some reason, I decided to kiss every single kid in the public schoolyard. I kissed boys and girls without discrimination. There was no sexual motivation behind my actions: it was hardly a Hollywood kiss anyway, just a peck on the cheek. But some of the boys immediately ran to the teacher or guard on duty and told of the atrocity that had been perpetrated upon them. It was sort of a twisted version of the Georgey Porgey nursery rhyme. Because only the boys complained, only half of the adventure was reported to Mr. Moore, the principal.

Mr. Moore called in my mother for a conference at which he bestowed upon me the dubious title of *homosexual*. I had heard this word, but every time I had heard it before, it was spoken in a derogatory sense about somebody else by one of my sister's boyfriends. This was the first time I had heard it applied to me. Mr. Moore based his "homosexual" theory on his belief that I had only kissed the boys, although in fact I had kissed everyone and homosexuality had nothing to do with it. (He may also have remembered that I dressed as a damsel for the school's Halloween contest.) When my mother told a neighbor about the conference later, I noted her quivering voice, and the clenched look on her face. The incident left a strong impression on me.

After Billy's family moved I developed a friendship with a new classmate named Bob Cote and I had feelings for him similar to the ones I had for Billy. Sex, however, was not a part of our relationship. In between catching toads, flying kites and swimming nude in a pond in the woods, sex never came to mind.

One night Bob invited me to sleep over. When I went I expected that we would just sit around and watch TV, but as the evening wore on I found myself becoming attracted to Bob. His mother, Mrs. Cote, had been keeping a close eye on us all evening so I waited until bedtime to make my advance. Before bed, I insisted on bringing my bed within a few feet of his. Once the lights were out I silently reached my left hand over to his bed and slipped it under his sheet and through his pajama bottoms.

Without a word Bob bounded from the bed and hurried out of the room. Where had he gone? Had I done something wrong by touching him? What was going to happen? These fears raced through my head. Soon I heard his Bob's mother open the door to the bedroom. I'll never forget the beating she gave me that night. I spent the rest of the night downstairs on the Cote's sofa.

I didn't tell my parents of the incident; I was afraid their reaction might be the same. For the first time, I developed an acute fear in my attitude toward sex. I had experienced physical pain because of my sexual desires. It was no longer tact that kept me from talking about sex, it was fear.

Bob and I somehow remained friends. My sex life did not stop but it slowed down a lot — mostly I just went back to undressing GI Joes and staring at them in privacy of my own room. I dropped out of the lavatory assemblage, which had continued since first grade. It was too risky; my fears kept me from enjoying the lavatory encounters so I just imagined them instead. I lost contact with the group but later heard it had grown considerably and was utilizing the bathroom facilities on the entire first floor including the auditorium and was working on a two-shift rotation schedule. But for me, that luxury had been stolen.

For years, my parents and I visited Provincetown, a summer resort on Cape Cod with a large gay population. My parents liked the area for its beauty: quiet Cape Cod Bay, rolling dunes, and quaint village shops on the only main street in town. Another wonder of nature was the homosexuals on every block of that main street. My parents occasionally commented on this but it never prevented us from vacationing there. Provincetown vacations provided something for me that Disneyworld and Williamsport, Pennsylvania did not. The sight of these women and men expressing love was subconsciously comforting to me. I never really related it to boy/boy girl/girl sex but it was a relief to see such openness.

In the summer after fourth grade, on the way to Provincetown, my mother took me aside for a talk. She warned that one day, a man in Provincetown might ask me up to his house. If I went up, terrible things would happen to me. The man might cut me up into little pieces. When I asked her why someone would do this to me she paused and said, "Because they are what you call homosexuals." She had no idea what impact that admonishment would have on me. She drove my ego to a really bad skid.

At this point, I was already conscious that I was a homosexual. Mr. Moore had said so. But a psychopathic killer I was not. Still, her fears helped me make sense of certain events in my past. My sister's freak-out at my admiring remarks about Batman. . . Billy's mother's quivering voice when she discovered us in the closet. . . the beating I received from Mrs. Cote. . . all inspired by the misconception that I, as a homosexual, was a psychopathic killer. I wanted at that moment to tell my mother that *I* was a homosexual and *I* wasn't the type to hack people into little pieces. I was just a nice kid. But to tell her would have risked an unpredictable reaction. What if she treated me like Mrs. Cote did? Restraint prevailed and I ended up more confused.

My attitude about myself got progressively worse from that day on. Until then, insulting remarks about gay people had no conscious effect on me because I didn't identify with the specific homosexual they were directed at. But now I was informed that *all* homosexuals were wicked and, knowing I *was* one, I instantly took it as a reflection on my personal character. I thought I was just a nice little guy who liked other little guys and would never hurt anyone in a million years. But apparently I was, in the eyes of my mother and many others, something more vile.

Of couse, my mother didn't realize how she had hurt my self-image. She had merely delivered a warning that she considered valid. How many parents deliver the same type of warning to their children and unwittingly create the same turmoil or confusion in their child's mind? For a child who is already aware of being homosexual, exposure to such attitudes can be traumatic.

Fortunately, even though being homosexual laid heavily on my conscience during fifth and sixth grades, *sex* was nevertheless still available. No feelings of guilt entered my mind when having sex with other boys because sex was something spontaneous, and a satisfaction of certain needs.

But there were other needs. Many of my feelings were stifled; there was no one with whom to communicate my innermost thoughts. Somewhere in my subconcious, fears were combining that would remain in my memory to haunt me later on. Would I be disliked? Was I dangerous? I was confused about my own identity. What did other people think of me? Did all the derogatory words I had heard such as queer, gay boy, sissy and pansy-face also pertain to me? I was not able to discuss these questions with anyone, so they sat in my mind to ferment.

Although I did my best to ensure that no one else knew of my homosexuality, I never deceived myself. I accepted my homosexuality. True, it caused me some mental anguish then and it would cause much more anguish in the not-too-distant future but I simply could not lie to myself.

Albuquerque Academy Library
6400 Wyoming Blvd. NE
Albuquerque, NM 87109

Withdrawal

My childhood years were secure in many ways. Our family never moved from Cumberland so I had a chance to feel settled in the town and meet many other kids. But I did not have enough time to secure myself for the traumas that were to come.

When I was twelve, the physical changes we had been told about in health class started to happen. I was getting taller, and growing pubic hair, and my voice was deepening a bit. It may seem impossible in contrast to the busy sex life of my childhood years, but I also developed a heightened sexuality. That was something we *hadn't* been warned about in health class.

One day after bowling with my father, he pulled the car into the driveway and told me to stay put a few minutes. His tone of voice indicated that a momentous subject was about to be raised. He asked me if I had felt any strange "tickling" when he had pointed out some of the natives during our vacation in Martinique. I wondered what the hell he was talking about. He asked if I knew where I had come from, and then filled me in on the raw truth about heterosexuality. I was awe-stricken. Then, for some reason, I began laughing hysterically.

The concept of heterosexuality did not immediately sink in. I didn't reject it, I just found it difficult to swallow. *This* was the alternative that had somehow eluded me through my childhood years. *This* was the thing that separated me from the beasts. Could this difference be the origin of all the pressure I was feeling? Surely it didn't have anything to do with me; I had no desire to try any of these heterosexual techniques. It all seemed like just conjecture; I didn't believe it could ever affect *me*.

Reality struck when Bob Cote began to talk about his interesting fantasies involving females. He seemed surprised when I had no comments to add to his discussions and instead stared blankly into space. At this point laughter was beyond me. I was afraid, but I also began to see a possible solution to the anguish I had felt. Maybe I could become heterosexual!

And so I began my efforts to make heterosexuality a reality for me. If it was going to make life easier then it would be worth the effort, and I put all my energies into the attempt. First I did some soul-searching. No help there. Nothing inside me had any inclination toward heterosexuality. Was it possible I was trying too hard? Could I be thinking about it too much? It was not so much that I feared being homosexual as that I was afraid of *not* being *heterosexual*. So I had to put all fears of my non-heterosexuality out of my mind. Still no success.

Finally, I began questioning Bob about his feelings. He couldn't really answer questions about why and how he had these feelings. My inquiries eventually led him to give me a copy of *Playboy*. I leafed through the magazine, not understanding how anyone but a professional contortionist would take any interest in the pictures. Did women actually pose like that or were the pictures taken with mirrors, lighting and special effects? Bob let me borrow the magazine overnight. I must have worn the pages thin trying to arouse the interest that I knew I would have felt if the photographs had been of men — but no dice.

As I entered seventh grade, I noticed that kids were changing physically as well as socially. No one looked like they had in sixth grade. Many of the boys grew facial hairs and the girls developed breasts.

Every day at lunch a group of my now-unrecognizable friends would assemble at one table. Intereresting conversations concerning heterosexuality occurred at nine out of ten lunches. What had happened? The kids I had once been so secure with in my sexuality had changed. They looked, sounded and smelled different. I was confused but didn't dare voice my thoughts because I remembered the aversion I had seen earlier in my life toward my sexuality. But back then, my friends had been like me. Now, unexpectedly, I was alone.

I managed to avoid trouble by not saying anything at lunch. Interestingly, Bob Cote and I began a sexual relationship. In fact, we had sex together quite frequently. So I was completely taken by surprise one day at the lunch table when he tried to initiate me into the conversation about heterosexuality.

"How about you, Aaron, what would *you* do if you had some pussy right now?"

I froze. For the life of me I couldn't think of anything original, which was the object of the discussion. All I could do was sit blank-faced through the most uncomfortable silence I have ever experienced. As the weeks wore on I tried to remain part of the group but I became more and more removed from these discussions until I was saying nothing all through lunch. When I started getting occasional stares and sneers from new members of the group, I felt it best to remove myself.

I sat alone at a separate table from that point on. Bob asso-
ciated with me at other times of the day but never ate lunch
with me. I asked him one day why he wouldn't sit with me at
lunch since we were best friends. He told me I acted too much
like a girl. Great! Girls were good for fantasies but he couldn't
eat lunch with somebody that acted like one. Confused again!

Meanwhile, my sister was getting married. I loved Cheryl
but with the eight-year age difference between us, we had
never been very close. She had dated boys a lot when she was
younger but I never really thought of her as a heterosexual.
Now I had to. Fortunately, I never had trouble with the idea of
people close to me engaging in heterosexual acts. I was able to
comprehend that my parents did it and I understood my
grandparents must have done it. What was difficult to handle
was the idea of the "Brady Bunch" parents or Beaver
Cleaver's parents involved in heterosexual activity.

My school life was becoming lonelier. Most of my former
friends ignored me. Bob and I stayed friendly and kept up our
sex life together, but many times Bob also talked about fantasies with females and salami. Bob felt guilty about having sex
with me and pretended that we never did. It was frustrating
because now, more than ever, I wanted to communicate with
someone about my sexuality — but there was no one available. Although Bob provided sexual stimulation, there was
little other communication between us; he was too inhibited.
In fact, one time he refused to have sex unless we first
hypnotized each other into being different people: he would
be a woman while satisfying me, and then we would switch. I
went along with it but felt ridiculous when the two identities
he had chosen for us turned out to be Ann-Margret and Jaclyn
Smith. My part was Ann-Margret, of course.

Bob and I had sex often yet there was always that suppres-
sive air. His attitudes wore off on me, and we both ended up

believing that what we were doing was wrong. I would have loved to communicate with Bob but under the circumstances any honest communication was inconceivable. I was afraid things would be that way forever, that the rest of my life would be lived in this state of suppressed tension. There was so much I wanted to express to Bob! Yet I couldn't, and faced with the need to keep my feelings from Bob, I soon began to deny those feelings even to myself.

I knew I was gay, and I knew that this was a gay relationship, and it scared me. Would relationships always be this way for me? Would I never be able to share my thoughts with anyone? I decided that this was what life would be like, and there was nothing I could do to combat it. Already I was coming to accept the fact that I was homosexual; now I would also have to accept the fact that being homosexual, I might never be able to communicate my deepest feelings with anyone.

Even with these shortcomings, my relationship with Bob helped keep me together. In retrospect, I can understand and sympathize with Bob's situation better. His parents were strict Catholics: Bob was always seriously punished for even the slightest variation from his mother's concept of normality. She once forced him to stand in a corner for hours when she caught him reading *Mad* magazine. Of course he refused to think about his homosexual feelings!

Bob's mother was a tall woman who reminded me of the bigfoot monster. She hovered over Bob, always suspecting him of some sort of mischief. She also suspected me of mischief, having never forgotten the incident with Bob years earlier. But with time she was again able to accept my presence in their household.

I began sleeping over at Bob's house again during seventh grade. His mother thought we enjoyed a perfectly platonic relationship in his room upstairs playing games and listening to Jim Nabors records — the only ones she allowed Bob to hear.

Little did she know that every night I slept over we would turn the record player loud and have sex to the beat of "Lord, You Gave Me a Mountain."

One night her curiosity must have been restless because she decided to hold an inspection. The record player was so loud that we didn't hear her climbing the stairs until she was halfway up. We had just a few moments to pull our pants back on. Bob's mother opened the door and to her surprise found us lying on the same bed. She tore off the sheets. We were completely clothed but that did not dissuade her from jerking Bob out of the bed and down the stairs, where he met a terrible fate with the belt. I didn't get beaten this time, but the mental pain and anxiety was worse than anything I had felt before.

Mrs. Cote called my parents to take me home. I don't know if she told them anything, probably she did not. Bob's parents put him in a Catholic school; they had once been friendly with my parents, but that friendship stopped. I tried to phone Bob once and they told me he wasn't allowed to associate with me any more. Now, homosexuality was connected not only with fear of physical pain but also with a fear of losing friends permanently.

The last holdout from my childhood sexual years was David Beamer. Dave was slower than other kids so he went to a special school. He and I never had a close relationship but once Bob was gone I turned to Dave in a desperate search for security and companionship. I began to frequent Dave's house and to have sex with him, yet our communication only became more diluted. The more I tried, the worse the situation got. It was torture because I wanted more out of these relationships than sexual stimulation. I wanted, yet I knew I couldn't have, all those things that went beyond sex such as communication and warmth. With Dave there was even less communication than with Bob.

Many days I went to Dave's house while he was working on

his motorized go-cart. There are few things in life that bore me more than go-cart engines. Yet every day I hiked down to Dave's house and stood in his garage watching him dawdle on pistons and spark plugs. Often we would not utter a word to each other for hours.

Obviously, we had no common interests anymore. Dave was more concerned with car engines than with relating to someone and sharing feelings. To talk about his feelings with me would threaten his self-image: to tinker with car engines did not. Yet Dave was still able to have sex with me, because it was a spontaneous thing like it is with most people.

I just wanted to be myself in the easiest possible way and at the same time to have friends. I was torn between these two desires. To conform would have been to surrender my natural feelings, but when I tried to be myself, people were scared away.

One day when I was at Dave's, I finally decided to talk about what I felt. I began by mentioning a recent television program that dealt with human relationships in a mature way. Dave did not enter the conversation, and it became a monologue as everything I had been harboring began to flow out. I told him how I felt different and alienated from him and everyone else. I told him I *did not* want to work on motorcycles and car engines and chain saws because that was not a part of me. I told him I wanted him to do something different. I begged him to stop acting as though those engines were a matter of life and death. I was addressing the part of him that wanted to preserve his conventional self-image. Not once did I mention sex.

Unfortunately, he viewed it as an assault on his refuge. He leaped up and kicked over the Honda he had been working on. He began stomping on it. He seemed to have gone wild. Then he stopped and looked at me with tears in his eyes and started screaming at me, "You *jerk*! You made me do that!" and went running into his house. I stood in his garage, bewildered. I hadn't realized the fire I was tampering with. The incident made me more confused. I didn't understand that David was under the same pressure I was but that he chose to deal with it differently. I did not see that *his* escape was conformity. In a few moments his father came almost running out of the house. He took one look at the bike and ordered me to leave their yard. David was never allowed to speak to me again. The next day I said hello to David when I saw him on the street. "Faggot!" he spit back

By this time I was fourteen, isolated from most of my class-mates and very lonely. The few friends I had in eighth grade were mostly girls and they were really more acquaintances than friends. Once in a while somebody would call me a faggot when walking past my lunch table. This was scary, because I thought I was keeping my homosexuality a close secret. I had hoped that no one knew or would suspect but apparently there were rumors. Fortunately, I heard these remarks only occasionally and only from a limited number of students.

In eighth grade I developed my first crush on a man from afar. It was an adolescent and purely physical attraction, but no less strong for that. The man was my eighth grade phys. ed. teacher. I always thought he treated me differently from the rest of the students: while the others were doing pushups I was allowed to walk the nature trail. I now wonder if he wasn't aware of the burden I was carrying.

Up until this time I had encountered prejudice from people who suspected I was gay, but never anything to give me absolute terror. Then, one day while sitting in science class, I happened to glance about the room and detect a fellow class-mate glaring at me. I overlooked it at first, but ten minutes later I noticed he was still staring. His name was Bill Quillar.

He must have been a quiet student because I had hardly ever taken notice of him before. I never saw him fraternizing with anyone else. He was a small student, not intimidating in size, but the look in his eyes was petrifying. He stared at me with an uninterrupted gaze that could melt steel. It was a look of complete disgust. I ignored him, but the next day he was staring again. And the next. . . and the next. . . and the next.

My mother sent me to Chomka's grocery market one afternoon to buy some milk. Rather than ride my bicycle on the street I decided to take a short cut through the woods. Halfway through, I saw two people standing in the middle of the path ahead. It looked as though they were shooting squirrels in the trees. A surge of fear rose in me when I realized that one of them was Bill Quillar, and he was holding what looked like a bb or pellet gun. I wanted to turn around as soon as I saw them but I knew they would come after me. There was no way I could avoid a confrontation.

As soon as they noticed me Bill lifted the gun, aimed and shot a bb at my leg. The pain made me stop my bike and get off. They ran toward me as I struggled to regain my composure and get back on the bike to ride in the opposite direction.

"Don't move, you queer!", said Bill in a slightly derogatory tone.

"Is this faggot a queer?" said the other person, who I didn't know and who probably came from another school. He was bigger than Bill and must have been a grade or two ahead.

"Yup, he's a fairy alright," said Bill condescendingly.

By this time I had seen the look in their eyes and I was frozen with fear.

"You are a fembot. And we don't like fembots. See that sign up on that tree, 'No Queers Allowed.'"

The big one punched me in the stomach when I looked up.

"Why don't you pick on someone your own size, like Russia?", I moaned.

"Get off the bike, scum!" Bill ordered.

When I refused to get off the big one sashayed over, punched me in the face, and pulled me off the bike. I was bleeding from my mouth. They ordered me to empty my pockets, then to take my clothes off and lie down on the side of the path. I had no idea what fate awaited me; instead of taking off my clothes I started crying frantically. They shoved and kicked me, then they both mounted my bike, fired a few last BB's at me, and rode away. I crouched on the ground in complete mental and physical agony, wondering how I would explain my missing tooth.

My world had crumbled. An attack like this would have distressed even the most secure teenager. For me, with the fear and suppression I was feeling, it proved to be the most horrible thing that could have happened. I was totally petrified. The most frightening thing was that when it was over, I had no one to honestly talk to about the indecency that had been perpetrated on me. I wanted so badly to run to my parents and tell them everything but that would have meant explaining just why these kids hated me. I was afraid of giving them any reason to suspect my sexuality. Although I could not be open with them, they were the only element of tenderness that existed in my life. I had no idea whether they could accept and love me if they knew I was different, or whether they would reject me. I couldn't take the risk of reaching out and finding nothing to hold on to. It was easier to lie, so I explained that I'd accidentally fallen off my bicycle onto a rock in the woods. My bicycle had been demolished. All the time I told this to my parents I bled inside, wanting to tell them the truth. Being torn constantly is bound to make you bleed somehow.

Things got worse. The attack left me filled with constant anxiety. How many more events like this would I have to endure during my life? It seemed so wrong that I should expect such maliciousness for the rest of my life simply because of who I was. I began to believe that everyone looked down on me and when anyone looked at me I thought I saw their seething hatred of me coming through.

When I entered high school I was completely isolated from the world. I had lost all concept of humanity; I had given up all hopes of ever finding love, warmth or tenderness in the world. I did not lie to myself, but I did my best to keep other people from thinking I was homosexual. For the most part I succeeded. I could not build a wall around myself as David had done but I could at least refuse to ever mention my *real* feelings. That way, I would never again suffer the consequences of being the individual I was.

I retreated into my own world. In an effort to distract myself from these problems I started writing and publishing a comedy magazine modeled after *Mad*, but my inner frustrations began to surface in the magazine's cartoons. The jokes had increasingly sexual overtones. *Wacky* built up a small circulation among my parents and family and a few school students, and the publisher of *Mad* even had a subscription and wrote me, "Dear Aaron, Watch yourself. *Wacky* is sometimes funnier than *Mad*." But my pent-up anxieties expressed themselves in the articles and finally my father and school officials labeled it pornography and ordered me to stop publishing *Wacky*.

With this outlet gone, the only goal left to me in life was to hide anything that could identify me as gay. I became neurotic about this. I once heard that gay people talked with a lisp. I was horrified when I discovered I had a slight lisp, and it made me self-conscious about how I sounded every time I spoke.

Self-doubt set in. I thought that anything I did might somehow reveal my homosexuality, and my morale sank even deeper. The more I tried to safeguard myself from the outside world the more vulnerable I felt.

I withdrew from everyone and slowly formed a shell around myself. Everyone could be a potential threat to me. I resembled a crustacean with no claws: I had my shell for protection, yet I would never do anything to hurt someone else. Sitting on a rock under thousands of pounds of pressure, surrounded by enemies, the most I could hope for was that no one would cause me more harm than my shell could endure.

This shell helped me protect my secret, but it could not protect my feelings from the prejudice I constantly encountered. In the long run my self-honesty would pay off, but for the time being, it caused unceasing mental anguish.

Meanwhile, my sex life ground to a halt. All of my former sex partners submitted to the demands of our heterosexual society, and many people I cared deeply about were torn away, leaving me alone at the bottom of an ocean too vast to comprehend. It was a realm of existence that, for me, held only loneliness, silence and the constant fear of being hurt.

In this state of permanent anxiety I needed some outlet, something to indulge myself in so I could forget about all these problems. The outlet I chose was not rock music, cars or pinball machines. It was worse. Food. I submerged in a world of nibbling, gnawing, gulping and swallowing everything in radar range. Each bite made me forget one more fear. I gained pound upon pound. I had weighed 140 pounds in junior high school but now, on entering high school, I weighed 190. I stopped weighing myself after that and just ate. Later — about twenty pounds later — food lost its cure-all properties. Yet I continued to gobble at a steamshovel pace. I created a vicious cycle between feeling depressed, then gorging myself, then feeling depressed again. My safety valve was open too wide. At the beginning of tenth grade I did weigh myself: At 5'7" I weighed 217½ pounds. I was dropping out of society with lead weights.

From all this it probably sounds like I had submerged in self-hatred and wanted to punish myself for what I was. I'm sure that was not the case. It was confusion, not self-hatred, that drove me to this escape. Confusion about where to turn, about what my future would be like if I couldn't fit into the rest of society. I wasn't *trying* to impose any punishment on myself. I was merely reacting to the doubts and fears that other people had forced onto me.

I knew no openly gay people. There was no one to tell me about gay literature. Cumberland had no gay organizations and my family had stopped vacationing in Provincetown a few years earlier. But early in the summer after tenth grade, at the height of my weight problem, my parents and I took a day trip to Provincetown. I was so withdrawn at this point that although the streets were lined with gay people, I found no satisfaction in their presence. Then. . . in the distance I heard a faint cry of many voices calling in unison. Soon the source of the noise came into view. A group of clean-cut people were marching toward us. At first, I could not read their enormous banner, but soon the words came into view: PROUD TO BE GAY. And they were chanting, PROUD TO BE GAY, PROUD TO BE GAY. I was astonished by the force with which they screamed their claim. Could these people really be "proud to be gay"? I wanted so badly to rush up to the group and chant with them, to cast away all my fears and. . . at that point my mother tugged my arm and said, "It's time to go home."

Did she see them? Did she know about the clean, happy homosexuals that had just paraded by? I couldn't bring myself to ask. If I did, she would surely have detected the enthusiasm in my voice and would be suspicious. I had lost too many of my friends already. I couldn't gamble on losing her love too.

I'm thankful now that I never tried to escape from my fears

through more self-destructive means such as alcohol or drugs. If I had, I'm sure I would have abused them badly.

There was a time, however, when I became curious about what alcohol was like. My father had a whole cabinet of liquor downstairs so one day when my parents had left the house, I decided to experiment. Nothing in the cabinet seemed attractive so I grabbed the first bottle in sight. It was whiskey. I mixed it with the only juice we had in the house then: prune juice. The drink was terrible but I managed to down four glasses of it. After those four glasses, I was quite honky-donky and could hardly walk. But my mind was free of the heavy thoughts that had constantly tortured me. I temporarily forgot my low self-esteem.

"Proud to be Gay!" echoed through my mind. Was it possible that gay people could feel proud of their individuality? I wanted to be in Provincetown at that moment, just to see these gay people and find out if the unity among them was real.

The alcohol had removed some of my inhibitions, and I reached for the felt marker on my bureau. I had to express the feeling that was emerging ever so faintly from somewhere inside me. I pressed the magic marker to the mirror and wrote, *Prood*. I grabbed some rubbing alcohol and a tissue to erase the *o*, and replace it with a *u*. The word *Proud* was now written on my mirror in bold black letters. I stood back and looked at it. Cautiously I approached the mirror again and wrote the words *to be*. Lifting the pen for the next step required more strength than anything I had done before. Under the words, *Proud to be*, I had just formed a capital *G* when suddenly my bedroom door was opened. I was so drunk I had not heard my parents return but now, standing in the door with an irritated expression, stood my father. He fixed his gaze upon me for a few moments, then turned and disappeared down the hallway. Quickly I picked up the tissue and rubbing alcohol and I erased the mirror, but I could not erase my fathers impressions. I felt like I had when Bob Cote's mother had discovered us. Was I going to be beaten again?

An hour passed and I dared not leave my room. I saw a police car arrive out front. Moments later the police entered my room and searched my drawers. They expected to find hidden drugs. They found none, but they ordered me to get ready for a ride. Apparently, my father thought I was on drugs and he interpreted the writing on the mirror as merely a bad trip. The open bottle of rubbing alcohol suggested that I was inhaling it and getting stoned. Relieved that my father had not suspected I was gay, and frustrated that I was being taken from my home, I offered no resistance and only cried.

The three days I spent in the juvenile rehabilitation center put me firmly back in the shell from which I had begun to escape. Confused and alone, my morale sank lower. Once I got out of the juvenile center, food became an even larger-scale problem than before, and I began constantly listening to the radio. I spent as much as eleven hours a day in my room, laying on my bed, calling the station whenever they gave out prizes.

School was merely a routine chore. I made no effort to pass any classes. My grades dropped as my weight increased. I had no friends, hardly even any acquaintances. I had hit the bottom of the ocean and I was sinking in the mud. Then came an unexpected lift. My telephone rang. Except for occasional wrong numbers and salespeople selling pottyseats, it was rare for my phone to ring. There was no response when I said, "Hello." The phone clicked as the person on the other end hung up. Five minutes later it rang again. Again the caller refused to say anything, and just clicked their phone rather than speaking. I hung up again.

The third time I decided to play along.

"Hello," I said. No response. So I proceeded with an entire discussion.

"Oh, hi! How ya doin?.... Really?.... That's wonderful. Really, oh what a coincidence because I was just swallowing goldfish too..... Excuse me.... Oh of course, live. I hate it when they die before they reach my stomach. It's no fun unless they wiggle a little bit in your intestines. Excuse me for one moment, I think I'm going to get one now...."

I gulped loudly.

"Mmmm, that sure was an appetizing goldfish. I wish I had a salamander chaser. Hey, listen, why don't you come over and we'll have a goldfish orgy."

I heard giggling on the other end of the line.

"Look," I said, "will whoever is there please identify yourself?"

The only sound was a click.

Suspecting that the caller was probably just shy, I soon set up a system of communication in which one click was a "yes" response, and two clicks were "no." Some people cannot communicate the same way other people do. I dubbed my new friend "the clicker." Soon I established that the clicker was a girl from my high school, and was in the same grade as me.

The calls continued for weeks. It was good to get calls from someone who actually wanted to communicate with me, even if they couldn't. When I wondered about this silence I named several possible reasons and the clicker, with a single click of the phone, agreed that she was shy.

Immediately a bond was formed. I could relate to that! And obviously the clicker liked me for who I was and didn't make any bad judgments about me.

After a while the clicker would actually speak "yes" or "no" and, finally, she would carry on conversations with me. Sometimes we'd talk for hours without running out of topics. Movies and television and pastimes dominated our conversations. We even developed enough trust to confide our problems to each other. To my surprise, I told her how concerned I was about my weight and it turned out she was also obese. We had many of the same difficulties in communicating with people and we both admitted that we felt lonely. The clicker had a part-time job in the mills after school, so she had no time to find friends, and a lot of the students looked down on her. She had seen me in school, she said, and thought I looked nice and kind — that was why she had first telephoned.

I didn't know the clicker's name or what she looked like, and I didn't care. She didn't feel comfortable identifying herself and said it was a superficial part of our relationship. That was fine with me. The clicker was being as honest as she could, and I didn't want to pressure her. After all, I knew what it was like to conceal a part of myself and to live in fear of being exposed.

After several months of a growing friendship I felt ready to bestow on the clicker the ultimate in trust. I had no doubt that she would handle it maturely. When I told her I was gay she said she was glad I told her, but she had sort of figured it anyway.

I was ecstatic to finally be open with someone. And she didn't freak out. There were no bad repercussions. I knew the clicker was not the real world, and that some people in the real world *would* freak out and hurt me, physically or mentally, because of who I was. I was not prepared for that yet. For now, it was wonderful just to realize that there were also people to whom I *could* turn to without being rejected. I was not yet ready to march through the streets of Cumberland with a PROUD TO BE GAY banner, but my outlook on the future grew a bit brighter.

My relationship with the clicker continued through tenth grade. We never had any physical contact. When we spoke on the phone, only our minds touched. We could have been ugly, beautiful, masculine, effeminate, black or white. Labels were unnecessary between the clicker and me.

By the time I entered eleventh grade, the clicker was calling less; finally her calls stopped altogether. She had never revealed her identity. I worried that she might be headed for a depression and was not secure enough to talk about it with me. Some day I hoped she would be ready to reveal her true identity, to other people and to herself, as she had helped me to do. But for now, all I knew was that the phone was once again silent.

And so, one of the closest friends I ever had was someone who I wouldn't even have recognized had we passed on the street. The clicker was there when I needed someone most. I will always love her dearly, for she touched a part of me that is rarely touched, by women, or by men.

Renaissance

When the Holocaust series was broadcast on TV, I was especially interested to learn that homosexuals as well as Jews were persecuted and put into Nazi concentration camps. Homosexuals were identified in the camps by a pink triangle they were forced to wear. It was good to see that somebody had begun to take notice, however briefly, of the atrocities committed against people like me.

Between the clicker and scraps of information like this, my self-confidence was improving slightly. I looked people in the eye when I talked to them, without always worrying that they would guess my secret. I knew that although I could not be completely honest with people at this point, there was some hope in others, so in the first month of my junior year I made a few new friends. As far as I knew, they were heterosexual, but they were good kids who didn't make any judgments about me. We didn't have too much in common, except that like me they all had some inner frustrations that they couldn't talk about. The camaraderie felt good, even though I could not share some of my deeper feelings with them, nor did they seem to share any of their hidden feelings with me.

Our group spent many evenings driving around Cumberland. One night it seemed that something illegal was going on. Everybody was filled with a nervous excitement. When I got in the car, I noticed a pile of rocks in the back seat; apparently we were going to break some windows. How exciting! All of us in the group had a lot of frustrations that we felt helpless to do anything about; I was as delighted as the others at the prospect of somehow relieving them.

We drove to a grungy building in town and cruised around it a few times until the street was clear. Then, on a signal, we all leaned out of the car and began awkwardly tossing the rocks, smashing several windows before driving off in frenzied laughter. Everyone was feeling good.

The next morning, I heard someone in the group bragging to another student that we had trashed the Gay Community Services center. I felt sick. I had had no idea. For me, like for the other kids, throwing rocks had been a release for thousands of frustrations, and the slight guilt I felt was easily ignored. I hadn't cared what we threw the rocks *at*. But for the other kids, there was no guilt at all. What guilt they might have felt about breaking windows was compensated for by the idea that we had attacked a *gay* building. I later learned that somebody had gotten their streets confused and we had been at the wrong building, but it didn't matter. I could not remain in the group after that.

Dropping out of this group didn't cause me the mental anguish I had felt during my earlier periods of isolation. The last time, I felt more as if the world had dropped *me*, and it made me lonely and depressed. This time *I* had chosen to drop out of the group for my own reasons. It didn't feel so bad.

I became active in the school drama club during my junior year, and I auditioned for the school musical *Oliver!* in

October. All I got was a part in the chorus, but it was fun to participate in the activity.

One day after rehearsals I stood in front of the school waiting for my father to pick me up. A tall, strong-looking kid began walking toward me from up the street. I took note of his physical characteristics because I wondered if I would have to run away from him. He kept walking toward me. He was coming straight at me. Was he going to bash me over the head with his books?

"Are you getting a ride home, Aaron?" he said to me.

"W-w-what?" I said.

"Are you waiting for a ride?"

"Uhh, uhh, y-y-yes, I believe so. How do you know my name?"

"Do you live near Benny's?"

"N-no, uh, I mean, yes. Why?"

"I was wondering if I could have a ride with you."

Something about him seemed nice. For one moment I forgot my fears and said he was welcome to ride with me and my father. An act of friendliness couldn't hurt, I thought.

He introduced himself as Paul and said we had shared a chemistry class in our sophomore year, and that was how he knew my name. In an effort to be friendly, I told him they were giving out concert tickets on the radio that weekend.

"I like rock and roll," said Paul, "but this Saturday I'll be at a National Gay Task Force meeting."

"A what?" I asked, wondering what the National Gator Force was.

"The National Gay Task Force," he enunciated. "I'm gay."

"Oh, really?" I was astonished by his nonchalance.

"Yeah."

"Funny, you don't smell gay," I joked, but I realized now that Paul had a certain freedom of manner that some people would call effeminate.

We both had a laugh and began a short conversation. I didn't notice my father driving up until his car had stopped in front of us.

"Egad!" I thought. I should have warned Paul not to utter a word while we were in the car, but it was too late for that now. Paul did do some talking once we were in the car, and I thought I would have a coronary thrombosis, but I didn't hear him say anything revealing. Sitting with Paul and my father, it struck me that for once in my life I was in a group where heterosexuals were in the minority.

Although I didn't hear Paul say anything on the way home that would give him away, my father apparently did. After Paul got out, my father turned to me and said "God, he is gay!"

I didn't answer, so my father started asking how long I had known Paul and how we had met. I made it clear that I didn't really know Paul at all.

But back in school, I began talking to Paul often. We had long conversations about what it was like for him to be gay. And yet, as much as I wanted to return his trust, I couldn't find the courage to tell Paul that *I* was also gay. My pipes had rusted and I couldn't flow. I had spent years looking forward to the day when I could say the words "I am gay," face to face, to another human being who would not reject me for it. Yet now that the opportunity was here, I could not do it.

Somehow Paul had freed himself of the fears and vulnerabilities that plagued me. He had an abundance of pride that he was more than willing to share. He never let people deprive him of the pleasures of life to which he was entitled. And his drive to express his true feelings was immeasurable: he had told his parents of his homosexuality a year earlier and then, when he had wanted to have his ear pierced, he had gotten his ear pierced.

Paul didn't go around screaming, "I am homosexual, hear me roar," at every chance, but he steadfastly ignored the stifling norms that surrounded us. He was sixteen and was already active in starting the Rhode Island chapter of Dignity, a gay Catholic organization. Paul was firm in his belief that gay is good.

Paul knew many facts about homosexuality. He told me that about 10% of the population is gay, and that gay people are basically no different from the rest of society. He was able to discredit so many myths and fallacies that I had heard and naively believed.

My self-perceptions began to change. In school one day, after I had known Paul for several weeks, he invited me over to his house. Paul was a little nervous when I arrived that evening. His parents were not home, and he asked if I would like to see some homosexual pornography. My blood pressure skyrocketed. I nodded and tried to conceal my enthusiasm as Paul pulled some periodicals from his dresser drawer. The first magazine he pulled out was not pornography; it was the *Gay Community News* from Boston, a newspaper that includes literature and play and movie reviews, so it was of some interest to me. But it must have been obvious to Paul that I was anxious to see some smut. He pulled out a few magazines that could satisfy my curiousity.

At this point, my hands were so sweaty they were sticking to the pages as I crept through each magazine. I suddenly realized how ridiculous this was. I had gone beyond the point of being dishonest; I was being farcical. A one-man situation comedy. It was time to save my integrity, so I turned to a now-smirking Paul and said, "If you haven't guessed, I'm gay too."

Obviously, he had suspected. In a few moments, we heard someone opening the front door. His mother stomped into his room with a look on her face that could melt an iron girder. She screamed at Paul and told me to get out of the house.

With Paul's help, I started to challenge all the prejudice I had encountered during 16½ years of life. Sure, it was scary to think that half my classmates might hate me if they knew my secret, but from Paul's example I knew it was possible to one day be strong and face them without apprehension. Many of my old ideas had to be discarded. My mother's warning that gays were psychopathic killers was based on ignorance, not on reality. The misfits were people like Bill Quillar and Bob Cotes' mother — not me.

I no longer felt self-pity, I felt anger: anger at a world that makes adolescence, which is hard enough for most people anyway, so much harder for people like Paul and me. Both of us were frequently subjected to verbal abuse; it was getting worse for me because I was now identified as Paul's friend. I was proud to be his friend anyway.

Paul never tolerated the barbs that were thrown at him. When he was called "faggot" he would always retort, "That's right, honey!" He never seemed affected by it all. Sometimes I feared for him because he got into bad situations by physically striking back when people hit or shoved him. But I gradually concluded that if being oneself meant being in trouble, then maybe being out of trouble was not such an important goal in life.

This gradual change in my mental attitude was reflected in my physical appearance. I no longer wanted an excuse to escape from the world; I wanted to be a part of it. I began attending weight loss lectures at the Slim Shoppe in Attleboro with my sister Cheryl. Cheryl was great in helping me stick to a diet and thus to recover from my social hibernation. As my attitude brightened, the 217 pounds I had carried around for so long began to drop off.

Paul told me that someday we would be understood as individuals. But that was in the future; for the time I was content just to be with Paul. It was a relief to be with someone from whom I kept no secrets, someone I could talk to about anything. We shared our feelings about everything from our experiences growing up gay to our futures as gay people. This feeling of complete openness was something new for me and was immensely fulfilling.

Paul and I began socializing frequently. He introduced me to his friends, most of them gay, but I never got as close to them as I was to Paul. Being independent, he didn't seem to have any great need of friends, but he seemed to welcome my company. He understood my situation and he gave me information or advice whenever I needed it. We spent more and more time together. My weight continued to drop, and my self-confidence grew. Life no longer felt so cold.

Gradually I realized that many of Paul's qualities, such as his resilience, were rubbing off on me. His strengths were my strengths. This companionship was exactly what I needed.

After several months of friendship with Paul, I realized that my feelings for him were unlike anything I had felt before. The sense of camaraderie was familiar from other friendships; the deep spiritual love I felt for Paul was new. So was the openness, the sense of communication with another. Those sexual escapades with neighborhood buddies had been nothing like this. All through my adolescence the shell which had protected me so well had also blocked all rays of warmth and love. But now that was changed. All the repressed love and warmth and kindness and strength were freed, all my thoughts and feelings were focused on one person. I was in love with Paul.

Paul and I were lovers in the true sense of the word; I felt as if we spent each waking moment together, either physically or in spirit. Life seemed significant again. I wrote poems for Paul; I looked forward to a future with Paul; I would write his name on a piece of paper and stare at it for hours.

Heterosexuals learn early in life what behavior is expected of them. They get practice in their early teens having crushes, talking to their friends about their feelings, going on first dates and to chaperoned parties, and figuring out their feelings. Paul and I hadn't gotten all that practice; our relationship was formed without much of a model to base it on. It was the first time either of us had been in love like this and we spent much of our time just figuring out what that meant for us.

Incidentally, I should explain that while I describe us as having been lovers, we never had a sexual relationship. Our love was a love of the spirit, and that was all I really needed at that time. Besides, I was now aware that society thought all sex should be reserved for a somewhat more mature age than 16½. And who was I to argue with social standards?

Meanwhile, I was getting closer to my parents. But now that I had friends to communicate with, I did not feel it necessary to tell my parents I was gay. It was not the time for that. I still had a residue of shame, but many of my earlier fears were gone because I realized now that I *would* have friends in life and I *would* have communication.

The Joy of Gay Sex is a book not unlike *The Joy of Sex*, but it includes illustrations and explanations of different techniques of homosexual sex. Paul had a copy and he loaned it to me one week. After seventeen years, I was surprised to learn there were techniques I didn't know!

Somehow, I accidentally left the book out on my bureau where my mother discovered it while housecleaning. Subconsciously, I may have been trying to let the cat out of the bag, but when she questioned me all I could say was that Paul forgot it at my house. The question was never brought up again. My mother had never liked Paul much and she now liked him even less. I took her reaction as a warning that it was still too soon to talk about my own homosexuality.

When Paul had told his parents of his homosexuality, they had totally rejected him. They were repulsed by his presence and said so to his face. Though Paul still had to live at home his parents avoided him; usually this meant they never came home except to sleep, leaving Paul alone most of the time. He was forbidden to have friends over, but with no one to check on him that rule was easily broken. I often went over after school, and many times even spent the night at Paul's.

One evening in October, when his parents did not come home at all, I slept over at Paul's while he was handling calls for the Gay Helpline. The Helpline was a service of the National Gay Task Force to help anyone who had a problem or question related to homosexuality. The phone company transferred calls to the phone of whatever volunteer was working each evening; thus, volunteers could handle calls right from their home. Paul's desire to help other gay people had inspired him to volunteer for the Helpline that evening.

I was excited at the prospect of learning something about myself by conversing with some of the callers about their questions and problems and doubts. Unfortunately, I wasn't much help. A lot of the calls were suicidal, and my positive gay feelings hadn't had time to become firmly rooted. Listening to potential suicides brought back too many recent memories. Paul was better at handling the most depressed callers.

I was put in charge of listening to the crank phone calls. And there were plenty. The anonymity of the telephone attracted cranks like flies to a soufflé. But Paul and I had the same anonymity: if the callers got too intimidating, we cheerfully told them about the unique uses of a telephone receiver.

One guy who called sounded so nice that Paul arranged to meet him. His name was Asher. When they met, Asher introduced Paul to his friend Jon, and eventually Paul introduced the two of them to me. I liked these new friends.

I had much in common with Jon and Asher. They were both sixteen and, like me, they had been through many crises because of social pressures. Soon after we met, Asher read a poem he had written. It pictured him as a stalactite hanging from the ceiling of a cave; when he could no longer cope with his self-doubts he crashed to the floor. Jon had tried to commit suicide several times during his adolescence. They had been friends since fifth grade, but until that year had never breathed a word to each other about their homosexuality.

Unfortunately, a feud arose between Paul and our two new friends. They saw Paul as a phony, constantly putting on airs about being Mr. Maturity. There was some truth in their complaints. Paul *did* speak of them as having undirected lives. He made catty remarks, saying "So, Asher, did you get a job yet?" and then saying, "it figures," when Asher told him he didn't have one. I could not identify with Paul's penchant for smugness, especially when he called Asher and Jon "bitchy queens." Why would one gay person pick on another's vulnerabilities? I ended up spending less time with Paul and more with Asher and Jon.

Paul and I still kept in touch. I could not stop loving Paul for the help he had given me when I needed it. And I found myself helping Jon just as Paul had helped me. Helping a gay person develop a positive self-identity is an opportunity that any gay (or well-informed straight person) should cherish.

Good fortune stumbled our way one evening when we went to a midnight showing of a film that embodied many of our feelings. It was *The Rocky Horror Picture Show*. When we went, I expected a thriller depicting a strange creature that threatened innocent people. That was something I knew I could relate to. What we saw was very different from what I had expected, but still something we could all relate to.

The movie dealt with such universal themes as interplanetary visitors, deflowered virgins, and sweet transvestites. It was a grand introduction to total openness and we loved it. What made *Rocky Horror* unique was that the audience became part of the performance by wearing costumes and dancing to the music. An amateur cast enacted parts of the film in front of the audience. The usual *Rocky Horror* costume was a waistcoat and spats for men and a corset and black fishnets for women. Or vice versa. It was an event where being yourself was acceptable, whether that was gay, straight, bisexual or cucumber freak.

Jon and I spent an occasional Friday or Saturday evening driving the 45 miles to Boston to see *Rocky Horror* at the Exeter Street Theater. We were curious to see how the Boston cast compared to the one in Providence. Returning from Boston one wintry Saturday we ran out of gas in subzero weather. The windchill factor was -20° and we were stranded between rural Cumberland and Woonsocket. We decided to hike in the direction of Woonsocket in hopes of finding a phone. Woonsocket Plaza was a few miles up the road; we would try hitchhiking if a car ever went by — which was not likely at 3:00 a.m. in rural Cumberland. To make matters worse, we both had all our *Rocky Horror* makeup on. As usual I was dressed as Riff Raff, a not-too-racy costume involving white face makeup and mascara. Jon, however, wore whiteface, bright red lipstick, heavy mascara, blue eye-shadow, eye-liner, and a beauty mark on his left cheek.

After twenty minutes of walking we saw headlights in the distance. We stuck out our thumbs, hoping the darkness would cover up our strange costumes. The car came to a halt. A moment later we climbed into a station wagon loaded with an average family of five. They had been on vacation in New Hampshire, the man explained, and had been interrupted by an unexpected emergency. There we were, with Mr. and Mrs.

Erma Bombeck in the front seat and their three children in the back with us, driving through Rhode Island at 3:00 in the morning. The woman kept looking at us nervously from the moment we got in, and after three or four minutes she told us to get out because they were taking the next turn. The man looked startled but pulled the car over anyway. We got out. The car drove out of sight without making a turn.

Jon and I walked on. Half a mile and several frostbitten toes later, we came to a phone booth at Woonsocket Plaza. It was as welcome as an oasis in the desert except that I had no change and Jon had only a fifty-cent piece.

We kept walking. After another half mile we came to an all-night Jack in the Box restaurant. Jon ran into the bathroom to wash off his makeup while I called the police for help. Fifteen minutes later a police car pulled up.

"So what do you want us to do?" asked the officer when we explained that we'd run out of gas.

"We'd appreciate it if you could give us a hand and help us get some gas."

The cop closed the window to confer with his partner while we stood freezing outside. Finally he re-opened his window and grudgingly told us to get into the car. He took us to a Sunoco station and an hour later, we got home.

In January of my junior year the school presented its production of *Oliver!* with me in the chorus. Asher and Jon attended. Asher even came to the cast party, but Jon was too intimidated by Cumberland High students because one of them made an insulting remark to him that evening.

At the cast party someone played the *Rocky Horror* album and everyone danced to a song called "The Time Warp." There was all sorts of booze around. By midnight Asher was so sick he hurried into the bathroom to throw up. I figured I could help him by cleaning up some of the mess, so I went in with him. Suddenly I found myself feeling sick too. My only choice was to throw up beside Asher in the same toilet. Absorbed in our misery, we didn't hear someone knock on the door. Then there was a louder knock, and someone bashed on the door, saying "Get the fuck out of there you fairies." I had automatically locked the door when entering the bathroom and now I was too sick to get up and unlock it. Asher and I said nothing. A boom echoed in the bathroom as someone tried to break the door down. Another boom. Finally the door flew open and some kid who wasn't even in drama club stood in the threshold. It was the same kid who had insulted Jon earlier. He took one look, said "That's disgusting," and ambled away. I never found out whether he was sick because of the smell, or because of our presence together in the locked bathroom.

Later that year I got a part as a cab driver in the school's production of *Harvey*. I decided to surprise our teacher and the other students by wearing fishnet stockings, high heels, a corset, a black cape and an afro wig to the dress rehearsal. No one, including my drama teacher, Miss Frappier, was bothered by this. They just saw it as a practical joke and did not equate it with homosexuality.

My life was getting happier on many levels. Only six months earlier I had known no one who was "proud to be gay." Now I had three close friends in Paul, Asher and Jon. I was discovering camaraderie, love, humanity, dignity, pride and emotional freedom, and I had friends with whom I could be open.

Paul and I had no classes together during the first half of our junior year. In February, we got an English class together: basic composition.

Since late autumn I had hardly spoken to Paul, and we rarely ran into each other in school. But now, Paul was clearly depressed over the disintegrating relationship with his parents. I tried to talk to him more and give him some support — to repay, if I could, all the help he had given me when *I* needed it.

Our friendship firmed up again. I realized that when you love a person you must accept their faults as well as their strengths. I was getting the education in personal relations that I should have gotten long before.

Paul began riding to school with me frequently. One day he told me he had been talking to a girl in his home room, who knew he was gay, and she suggested that he go to the junior prom with a guy. Then he asked,

"Do you wanna go?"

"Okay," I said, "but I'll never have time to buy a gown."

Paul didn't laugh.

I realized that Paul was serious. He began talking about how he had the right to go to the prom and that there was no one who should be able to stop him. I completely agreed. But for me it would be too big a step, too soon, to be his date. I told Paul that no, at that time I could not accept his invitation to attend the prom.

I had a sinking feeling that this wasn't the right time for Paul, either, but he insisted that with the help of his local gay activist friends he could pull it off. He asked Mr. Lynch for permission to attend the prom with Ed Miskevitch, a Brown University student who led the gay youth group there. When Mr. Lynch denied him permission, Paul received help from Chuck Noice of the National Gay Task Force. Unfortunately, since Paul was only seventeen he could not take the case to court without parental support, and his parents of course refused to back him.

The newspapers latched on to the story and soon the whole state was aware that a high school student wanted to go to the Cumberland junior prom with a homosexual date. Paul got threatening phone calls at home, and the school offered him protection in class. I gladly gave him a ride to school every morning since he no longer felt safe on the bus.

Subsequently Chuck Noice, who had tried to help Paul, had a hard time in his search for a job. Employers found reasons not to hire him. It is sad that someone could be punished for his willingness to stand up for human rights.

By the end of the school year Paul's relationship with his parents had completely dissolved. They made it unbearable for him to live at home. This act of ostracism appalled me. Something is radically wrong when a seventeen-year-old high school student can lose his home, his family, and all traces of security, because he refuses to hide his real feelings.

Cumberland students misinterpreted Paul's efforts to attend the junior prom. They believed Paul had lost a battle and that prejudice had triumphed over individual freedom. In fact, Paul was never even able to fight. There was no loss or victory, only a victim: Paul. I was disgusted by this un-American attitude on the part of the students. Where was their sense of fair play?

Paul decided to spent the summer of 1979 in New York. Jon, Asher and I made plans to live there during the summer also. Jon and I ended up staying together at the YMCA.

Many times that summer Paul and I met and had long talks while walking in Central Park. We even marched in the protest against *Cruising*. Confused and upset by the split from his parents, Paul appreciated having a friend around. I was proud that Paul could show such strength after his ordeal.

I was sorry to leave Paul in New York when fall came, because I knew he would need me now more than ever. The city can amplify feelings of loneliness and I wanted to be with Paul when he needed a friend. We agreed to correspond during the winter.

Top left: I pose with a copy of Wacky in the middle of my sophomore year.

Top right: My senior class picture, taken just before the beginning of my senior year.

Lower right: A photo taken shortly after the prom.

Senior Year

On the first day of my senior year, Mr. Lynch gave his usual address to the senior class. As the seniors, he told us, we must set a good example because our younger classmates looked up to us.

In his next breath, Mr. Lynch told us we were all going to have a good year, because we no longer had to put up with "the problem" of the year before. He was referring to Paul, of course, who had stayed in New York and would not be a Cumberland student this year. Everyone in our school was now presumed to be heterosexual. At least, Mr. Lynch felt sure that no one in the school would have the pride to be openly gay.

After this demagogic speech, the students went wild. Most of them would have forgotten their earlier feelings about Paul but Mr. Lynch was not satisfied with that. He wanted the students to believe that there were no more homosexuals in the school, that we were now somehow spartan and pure. To him, Paul was the problem. He saw nothing wrong with the prejudice and hatred that he was instilling in the students. It is sad that for decades people like him have set such bad examples for students and no one said anything about it.

I vowed that my final year in Cumberland High would be different from all my previous years in school. Before, I had only seen prejudice directed at *me*. Now I saw it directed at someone else, and I saw it as nothing more than fear and ignorance. This new perspective made all the difference for me: I was apprehensive about facing the other students as an openly gay person but I would do it anyway. I was sure that I *could* overcome their homophobia. From now on I would be able to look at prejudice in a new light, even if it was directed at me, and to see that since it is merely ignorance, it meant nothing to me. I would not advertise or flaunt my homosexuality, but I *would* be open about it.

The assembly was dismissed. I was surprised to see a familiar face across the room. It was Bob Cote. He was back from Catholic school. His physical appearance was different after four years: he was bigger, and well-built. As I walked toward him I noticed a girl, Beatrice Duvwalge, hanging on to his left arm. I only knew Bea slightly, and she had never been friendly to me. When I got to them I said, "Bob. . . . Long time no see!"

Bob stared forward, ignoring me. "Get lost, agfay," Bea replied to me in pig Latin.

I was shocked. Somehow, in the years Bob was away from me, he had come to believe that our friendship meant nothing. Now he was afraid to even say hello. I suppose that for Bob, stifling his personality seemed safer than living with the consequences of emotional freedom. Now he was hooked up with Bea, who knew his vulnerabilities and acted as a defense against his true feelings and his real bisexual self.

During the first few days of school I got acquainted with my new classes and classmates. I could see that my worst class would be biology. The kids made many wisecracks at me but I ignored them as usual, realizing that nothing they said was important, and nothing I could say would make any difference.

In October, tryouts were held for the school's production of *A Thurber Carnival*. The play consisted of dramatizations from various James Thurber stories. I auditioned for the role of first man, which included the character of Walter Mitty. Mr. Mitty, rather than cope with reality, fantasizes that he is a surgeon, a World War II pilot, a secret agent. . . . Many kids wanted the role. I was thrilled when I received it.

In phys. ed. I was taunted as much as ever. Students called me "cocksucker" and occasionally slashed me with wet towels in the locker room. It was a small group of jerks who made the most trouble and they were so irrational that nothing I could say would change their opinions. I think it is always a small minority that makes life harder for anyone who is different. Most kids, left to themselves, wouldn't have cared what I was as long as I didn't bother them.

When I returned from gym to find a wad of spit on my clothes, I decided it was time to see Mr. DeGoes, the vice-principal. I told him what was happening and asked if it would be possible for me to transfer to an extra drama class rather than take phys. ed. When he said I could be transferred I was relieved. Mr. DeGoes explained that Paul had been able to transfer out of phys. ed. the year before when he told him that he was gay. (Paul never told me about that!) I was about to tell Mr. DeGoes that I was gay also but he said, "Of course, we'll have to tell your mother and she'll have to come in with you tomorrow morning."

I stopped dead in my tracks. To tell my mother of my homosexuality at this point would give her all the wrong impressions. When she heard about the cruel treatment I received in phys. ed. she would believe that gay life could

never be happy. I wanted her love, not her pity. Pity is a
natural reaction to the plight of gay youth but I did not want
my mother to form solid opinions about gay life without hearing the entire story of how prejudice can be transcended and
gays *can* live happy lives. At this point, I did not feel I could
relay that message well enough.

I said nothing and walked out of Mr. DeGoes's office. Now I
realized the vicious thing that Mr. DeGoes was doing to me.
I would not tell my mother and he probably knew that. I
wonder if Mr. DeGoes offered that same alternative to heterosexual students who were harassed and came to him for help?

In desperation, I turned to my phys. ed. teacher and begged
her to let me take my classes after school so I would not be in
such anxiety. She refused. But when the time came to choose
a new phys. ed. class I took one with a different teacher. I told
him my story — he was more helpful and agreed to release me
from class a few minutes early so I could change clothes
without trouble. I was still hassled occasionally but it was the
best I could do for the moment. And whenever the chance arose, I
skipped phys. ed.

November of my senior year rolled around and some teachers were still making jokes about Paul. It was homophobic
humor such as, "Thank God, we only have fruit cocktail in
the cafeteria now instead of in the classroom." It was a blatant
display of prejudice and it sickened me.

Asher and I were in Providence after *Rocky Horror* early in
December so we stopped at Mike's Diner in Kennedy Plaza to
get a few hot dogs. Kennedy Plaza has a circular roadway
where many heterosexuals drive around trying to find someone to have sex with. After buying the hot dogs we drove
around Kennedy Plaza and saw many gorgeous men through
our peripheral vision. (Looking them directly in the eye

would have been too risky and broken the cardinal rule against cruising straight men.)

Neither of us was tired so we drove around the city a while longer. As was our custom when we cruised, we explored every nook and cranny of the city that my car would fit in. Then we stumbled upon a parking lot. I had seen the Metropolitan Parking Lot by day, but it was nothing like *this*. People were driving cars all around and we soon realized that they were homosexual men, driving around trying to find someone to have sex with. We even saw a few of the heterosexual men who we had just seen in Kennedy Plaza, but no women. We knew we would return, but now it was getting late so we headed home.

Later that month, when I drove up to my house one evening, I found the word GAY spraypainted on the outer storm door of my house. Bewildered, I hurried in and asked my mother if she had written anything on the front of the house. I should have kept my mouth shut because, of course, she hadn't, and she hadn't even noticed it was there when she drove into the garage earlier that evening. I found some paint remover and took the paint off the glass. I was not ashamed of the word "gay", but I did object to people defacing my house! Homosexuality is only one facet of my personality. The label "gay" cannot possibly express all my inner facets, only the one that is most misunderstood.

I made a new friend in my senior environmental science class. Anne Guillet never showed any prejudice because of my sexual preference, and we developed a friendship through a steady exchange of notes in class. We shared many of our thoughts with each other despite our radically different sexuality. Another person who never cared about my sexual preference was my friend Jon Miosky. Jon often spent a Friday or Saturday evening at *Rocky Horror* with my gay friends and

me. My heterosexual friends like Jon and Anne all knew that
I was gay during my senior year. I was open with anyone who
asked about my sexuality.

Jeff Endign, a junior, approached me while I sat in a
secluded part of the library one day. We no longer shared the
drama class that we had been in the year before. He sat down
beside me and I knew there was something on his mind. He
told me that someone had tried to force him to indulge in a
homosexual act in the woods. It happened when he was
hitchhiking and some man picked him up. He seemed upset
so I gave him the Gay Helpline number. He said he would call
them and then, completely unexpectedly, he said, "Give me a
blow job." I thought I'd die, especially as he started to unzip
his pants. The space was secluded, but not *that* secluded. I
felt embarrassed for two or three seconds and turned my head
the other way. When I turned back he had disappeared.

Paul and I corresponded occasionally. He wrote mostly
about the hassles New York life posed for him. He did not
always communicate that well on paper but I could read
between the lines: he did not seem happy there. Eventually,
we discontinued our writing but still I could not stop caring
about his well-being in the bowels of New York City. I missed
Paul very much.

Asher and I wanted to return to the Metropolitan Parking
lot (which we now called the Metro). We arranged to meet
one evening on the small bridge over the Providence River. As
I stood waiting for Asher, a man in a dingy Volkswagen drove
up beside me. "Twenty-five dollars," he said. I shook my
head. I was astonished that anyone would pay twenty-five
dollars to have sex with that frumpola. I reported the incident
to Asher when he arrived with Jon. They opened my eyes to
the fact that *he* had been offering *me* twenty-five dollars. I
was very naive about the fundamentals of prostitution at the
time. Like me, Asher and Jon were new to this center of

gay cruising but they did understand the idea of prostitution.

Still, even they were surprised by the vivacity of action going on. All of us were taken by the place — although Jon was disappointed that only fifteen men had tried to pick him up on his way through the parking lot.

We soon met some young men who were hustling. This was something they seemed to enjoy and I saw nothing wrong with it. Such a profession is open to men and to women; the only sad thing is when people are forced into it because they have no alternatives.

Our new friends told me that the frumpola who had tried to pick me up was actually an excellent playwright and poet. I was ashamed that on first sight I had labeled him as a loser. How many times had I suffered when other people labeled me?

We spent many fun-filled nights down at the Metro. None of us knew exactly what drew us back time after time. We rarely were picked up by anyone, it was just fun to sit in the parking lot and talk.

Each of us ran into someone we knew who suffered from a severe case of closet syndrome. I ran into one of my grammar school teachers and we had a pleasant discussion. But the strange thing was the first sentence he said when he saw me: "Well, Aaron. I knew I was bound to see you here sooner or later." Hmm.

Every day in school I sat in the library during my free periods and read play scripts. In the middle of reading *Night of the Iguana*, I saw some spit drop onto one of the pages. I turned around and Jeff Endign was standing there. "That's my come," he said. Ugh! I saw the terrible way that some people have to stay in the closet in Cumberland and turn all their sexual energy inwards. When I asked Jeff to sit down and talk to me he quickly walked away again.

I met other gay people in school but they were so closeted that when they tried to tell me they were gay, most of them couldn't. One day they would say they were straight, the next day they would be gay and the next they would be bisexual. I could see that Cumberland did not enccurage freedom of individuality and that I was not the only person who was suffering because of this atmosphere. I always gave these kids the Gay Helpline number but I sincerely doubt that any looked into it.

Asher, Jon and I were so enthusiastic about *Rocky Horror* that we formed our own cast and performed it in Newport at the Jane Pickens Theater. Weekend after weekend we performed in front of the screen during the movie. I always played Riff Raff, a servant. A new friend, Jeanne, began driving to Newport with us.

Jeanne is a black friend of mine who, at six feet and 290 pounds, is intimidating to people who don't know her. Jeanne has a beautiful easy-going personality and we loved her. She attended every show with us at midnight in a suit and bow tie.

At *Rocky Horror*, I often had the sensation of several beady eyes staring at me as I sat in the theater lobby with the rest of the cast. Most us were dressed in a black suit, tie and spats, with a few people in drag or dressed more bizarrely.

When the queer bashers gave us a hard time, Jeanne could often intimidate with them with her size alone. In the early days we could stick around the theater after each show to change out of our costumes, but the manager began to get annoyed at the delay so we started wearing our costumes home. It was a ten minute walk from the theater to my car and in full costume, it wasn't always a pleasant stroll.

One Friday night, four people followed us from the theater. They were men around twenty and they walked behind us hollering, "Hey, sweetcakes. Hey, chicky-chicky," and

Joseph F. Hussey

The Rocky Horror cast — Jon is standing third from the left, and I'm kneeling second from the right.

making sarcastic sucking noises at Jeanne. We kept walking, figuring it was best not to egg them on by lowering ourselves to their level. They kept following. What were we going to do? I could understand the predicament that many women face in today's society.

And then, completely unexpectedly, Jeanne swivelled around, ripped open her blouse exposing her huge breasts and screamed, "Whooooooaaaaaaahhhhhhhhh!!!" We jumped into the car and sped off as they crouched in laughter. As we drove by we bombarded them with marshmallows — leftover props from *Rocky Horror*.

We escaped these jerks but *Rocky Horror* did not. It was cancelled soon afterward because of the damage these homophobics sometimes did to the beautiful Jane Pickens Theater by ripping up the seat cushions.

School was less stifling now that I had come out to all my close friends and anyone else who bothered to ask. But a few classes were still hell. The torment continued in phys. ed. and I skipped class more often. My former gym teacher (the one who had been so unhelpful before) caught me in the hall one day and she hauled me in to Mr. DeGoes's office.

Mr. DeGoes told me that because of my excessive truancy from phys. ed. and my frequent tardiness in the morning, he had to suspend me. But a regular suspension was too light a disciplinary action for me. I would receive *in-house suspension* instead. This meant I would spend three school days sitting in one room with twenty other delinquents.

I appealed this sentence to Mr. Lynch. I did not know Mr. Lynch; as principal, he maintained a certain mystique. Mr. Lynch always reminded me of the Queen of England when he paraded through the cafeteria or down the hall, occasionally with Mr. DeGoes at his side.

I walked into Mr. Lynch's office and told him in ten words

or less why I had been skipping phys. ed. He was indifferent to my story. Then I glanced about the room and saw several sports trophies. Now I could see why he had no sympathy for someone who skipped phys. ed.

I am convinced that in-house suspension was designed for hardened criminals more than for high school students. It consisted of sticking twenty or more students in an empty room for the entire school day. Usually, a teacher was there to play babysitter/prison guard, and the inmates of in-house supension would take out their frustrations by spitting on the teacher. But during my confinement, the students found a better target: a living, breathing human target that they could *justifiably* spit on, without fear of repudiation.

And spit they did. All their frustrations with the administration were channeled toward me. Every minute of in-house suspension seemed like an hour of torture.

When I complained to the teacher in charge I was allowed exactly two minutes in the lavatory to clean my back of spit and other foreign matter. For each minute I spent in the bathroom over two minutes, it meant an extra day of in-house. I got back to the room within two minutes.

One person I met before the Newport *Rocky Horror* closed down was Geri McGowan. She and I remained close friends after Rocky Horror ended in Newport. She slept over at my house many times and my parents began to think she was my girlfriend. I tried to convince them she was not, yet they persisted in razzing me with jokes and innuendoes about Geri. The years that I had been completely introverted they now dismissed as my shy years. They must have felt I was a late bloomer when I began showing up with girls at age 17. Of course, my male friends visited me too. My parents even suspected that some of these friends were homosexual but considered them to be no influence on me — "Thank God!"

Parents can be blind to signs of gayness in their own children though they would immediately see such signs in others. One time my father told me Jon was so "obviously gay" that there was no way his parents couldn't know. I wanted to tell him then. I wanted to say, "How can you be so blind? I'm gay too and *you* don't know it!"

I didn't. This would be the wrong time — I would merely be saying it to prove a point. When I did tell my parents I was gay I wanted it to be because I loved them and felt they should know.

I liked Geri a lot and had as much fun with her as with my gay friends. We never had to restrict ourselves when going out. If I wanted to go to a gay bar that was fine with her, and I often went to straight bars of Geri's choice.

A bar we went to frequently was Lupo's, in Providence, which had a largely heterosexual clientele. I always had a good time there and even met some nice gay people at Lupo's. The one thing I don't like about gay bars is that you almost never meet nice straight people in them.

I decided to show Geri a little of what homosexual cruising was like by taking her over to the Metro. I parked when we got there and we sat in my car. The lot was crowded and Geri was awe-stricken. After about fifteen minutes, cars began slowly filtering out of the lot. Soon only four cars were left. Then a car pulled up beside ours and the person inside said, "Get the fuck out of here."

"Perhaps if you ask us politely," I said.

"I ain't gonna ask you to do nothing you fucking queer." The guy looked infuriated and he stepped out of his car with a now-familiar expression of nausea on his face. He held something in his hand.

"If you want us out, you'll have to make us," I said, screeching the tires and driving in a circle around him.

He ran to his car and began following me. I led him out of

the lot, into Kennedy Plaza. I picked up speed, but so did he. I drove out of Kennedy Plaza toward the east side. He was still close on my tail. Then in my rear view mirror I saw him take a left turn. I thought we had lost him until I went around another circle onto South Main Street and saw him stopped at a red light at the bottom of Waterman Street. Between me and the light was a tunnel that buses use as a quick route to the east side but from which cars are prohibited. My car screeched to a halt behind his, giving me direct access to the tunnel.

He got out of his car, a crowbar in his hand. I decided to escape via the tunnel. I had always wanted to drive through this "buses only" tunnel, but never would have guessed I would do it under these circumstances.

My school grades were improving this year. English was my favorite subject, except I didn't realize just how homophobic my English teacher was. One time, his assignment for the class was to write a report on anything that interested us, with an emphasis on something that affected everyone.

This, of course, meant boys would report on baseball, car engines and female movie stars, and girls would report on gardening, sewing and male movie stars. I chose homosexuality as my topic, and spent a month working on my report. When I handed it in, my teacher ripped it up. It was improper subject matter, he said. I had had just about enough.

During lunch one day, Bea Duvwalge called me to come over to her table. "Aaron," she said, "Has anyone asked you to go to the Sadie Hawkins dance?"

Her friends started giggling so I knew she wasn't serious.

"No, Bea," I replied.

Bea had a habit of ripping open her milk carton and dipping her Hydrox in the milk until it was saturated.

"I didn't think so," said Bea. "No girl wants to be *that* safe." With that she smugly inserted a soggy Hydrox into her mouth. Her friends looked on giggling and she laughed too.

Biology class had been bad all year, but in about March it got worse. One day several students began hassling me when the teacher walked out of the room. First they just indulged in verbal taunts, but then it escalated. If this had happened in my junior year, I would have sat there and pretended to read poetry, but I was no longer willing to accept this treatment. They were throwing dissected animal parts at me.

I walked out of the class to the school office. I knew that I had to make the school administration deal with my situation because conditions were not getting better and I felt the school had a responsibility to protect the rights of each student.

When I got in to speak to Mr. Lynch I told him what had happened. He said, "Well, that's to be expected considering that your classmates are aware of your friendship with Paul Guilbert." I had never told Mr. Lynch of my friendship with Paul Guilbert! I had never spoken to him at all except for the few minutes when I appealed my in-school suspension to him, and I rarely even *saw* Mr. Lynch. And what effect did my friendship with Paul have on the torment I was receiving from these students, anyway? Was prejudice justified because of my association with a homosexual? Or did my friendship with Paul prove that I was a homosexual also? I *had* had enough.

The Decision

In April, Mr. Lynch held the traditional pep talk to jolt the graduating class out of senioritis. Just as he had done the previous autumn, he referred to the "problem" that had existed at the 1979 prom. Naturally, the students exploded in enthusiasm. I wanted to stand up and scream, "I am gay and proud and will not be oppresed!" I was determined that Mr. Lynch would not go on forever stirring up this prejudice in the hearts of my fellow students. But for the time, discretion prevailed. Besides, I valued the use of my two legs.

Everyone buzzed about the prom after Mr. Lynch's speech. The girls planned to make or buy their gowns. Some guys reminisced about last year's prom. But like always, I was left out of these discussions. Through all of my high school years I had been left out and I was tired of it. I wanted to be part of the group like all the other students.

The simple, obvious thing would have been to go to the senior prom with a girl. But that would have been a lie — a lie to myself, to the girl, and to all the other students. What I *wanted* to do was to take a male date. But as Paul had shown the year before, such honesty is not always easy.

There was an important difference between Paul's case and mine, though. Paul had not been able to fight for his rights because he was seventeen at the time. I was now eighteen and legally able to make my own decisions. If I wanted to go to the prom with a male escort and the school tried to stop me, I could take the case to court.

But should I do that? This would require much thought if I was to make a decision without being selfish, uncaring or irrational.

If I went to the prom with another guy, what would be the benefits? For myself, it would mean participating in an important social event and doing so with a clear conscience and a sense of wholeness. But how would it affect the rest of the people involved?

I believed that those who had themselves faced discrimination or prejudice would immediately understand what I was doing and its implications for human rights. There would be others who may never have had direct experiences with prejudice but who would recognize my right to the date of my choice. These people may have been misled to believe that homosexuality is wrong, but they could still understand that my rights were being denied.

At the opposite end of the spectrum were the homophobics who might react violently. But the example I set would be perfect for everyone. We would be just one more happy couple. Our happiness together would be something kids could relate to. I would be showing that my dignity and value as a human being were not affected by my sexual preference.

I concluded that taking a guy to the prom would be a strong positive statement about the existence of gay people. Any opposition to my case (and I anticipated a good bit) would show the negative side of society — not of homosexuality.

To attend the prom with a girl would not be unenjoyable but it would be dishonest to my true feelings. Besides, most kids now knew I was gay. If I went with a female, I would probably have received more taunts than from going with a male. By going with a male I would win some respect from the more mature students, and I would keep my self-esteem.

I tried not to worry about the possibility of violence. Certainly I would face opposition. It was inevitable given the rampant prejudice against homosexuals today. But the threat of violence was not enough to change my mind, since I encountered that every day to some degree. Perhaps such threats would diminish in the future as people saw more homosexuals participating openly in everyday life.

My biggest concern was for my parents. Although the entire student body and administration of Cumberland High School knew or assumed I was gay, my family had remained blissfully blind to this reality. The news could be heartbreaking to them. Plus, it might get them ostracized by the neighbors, banned from town social gatherings. . . from church. . . from Tupperware parties! Was I willing to take this risk? No! As much as I believed in my rights, I valued my relationship with my parents too much to have it abruptly severed. After all, for years I had hidden my sexuality for fear of losing my parents' love. As a child it had been *the* most important thing to me. Now, as a man, it was just as important as before. I wanted to go to my prom, but it was not as important as eighteen years of love.

I decided to tell my parents of my homosexuality first, then ask them how they would feel about my going to the prom. If it seemed like too much for them to accept, I would forget the prom and just be happy that I no longer had to be secretive with my parents. But if they rejected me merely because I was gay, then I would still pursue my rights, even at the prom, realizing that my parents were good people but were horribly misled.

Until now, I had never spoken to them about my homosexuality. Like many adolescents I had drifted away from my parents lately. Now I had an impetus to improve my communication with them. I decided to approach my parents separately; a thousand times I rehearsed what I would say.

It began "Ever since I was a kid. . ." and ended, "I hope you love me enough not to reject me." But when the moment of truth came I felt more self-confident and said, "I don't know if you've had any suspicions, but I'm gay."

Long pause. My mother replied, "I'm so glad you were finally able to be honest with me." She had long suspected. My father had not; when I told him he broke down and cried. Yet they both loved me unconditionally. When I explained why I wanted to go to the prom they were supportive. I was my own man, they each said, and I would have to make my own decisions.

It felt great to be able to talk to my parents about this. Their reaction was encouraging and I decided to go ahead. I would invite Paul Guilbert to the prom.

Anne Guillet wrote me a note in environmental science class when I asked for her advice about the prom. She wrote:

Dear Aaron,

Last year, Paul's attempt to bring a guy to the prom was seen by most people, in fact I think by all, as a grab at publicity. That was because no one knew Paul, he just showed up out of a clear blue sky (and raised a ruckus). Since you've been in Cumberland much longer and have more close friends, people won't suspect you of such ill motives so easily, but this is what they will think.

1. Paul made you do it.
2. You're crazy.

3. You believe in gay rights.

In that order. Now *I* know you did it for reason 3 but you should think about how other people are going to react and I think you should make an effort to explain what you believe. I respect any decision you make, as long as you really think about it carefully.

Love,
Anne

I took her advice and painstakingly wrote a letter to the school newspaper, explaining why I decided to go to the prom with a male date. The letter said that I hoped no one would be hurt by what I was doing, that a victory in court would be a victory for every Cumberland High student because it would be a blow against prejudice. The next issue of the school paper had space for all sorts of trivia, but my letter never appeared.

Later in April, the school theater group took its annual bus trip to New York City. Our teacher, Miss Frappier, was an exceptionally warm and friendly person and we were a tight-knit bunch — one of those rare groups of thespians whose members had no pent-up distrust or jealousy toward each other. On the bus Miss Frappier gave out the spring awards; I received one of them, for an outstanding performance in *A Thurber Carnival.*

In New York we went to the Guggenheim Museum and to a Broadway production of "They're Playing Our Song"; then when the group returned to Rhode Island I stayed in New York to spend time with Paul.

Paul seemed to be getting happier in the city. Our friendship had not faded although Paul and I had not seen each other for months. We took a long walk through the Village, bringing each other up to date on what we'd been doing, and enjoying the feeling of the trees in bloom and spring in the air.

By evening I had settled any doubts I still had about who I wanted to invite to the prom. And so, with sweaty palms and butterflies in my stomach, I finally asked Paul: "I was wondering, um, do you have a date for the Cumberland High prom this year?"

Paul began laughing. "I'd love to attend the senior prom with you," he finally said. My feeling of happiness lasted all the way back to Rhode Island.

In Cumberland, prom tickets were on sale. Rather than go through the motion of trying to buy a ticket in the cafeteria, where they would want the name of my date and would refuse to sell me the tickets anyway, I went right to the main office and asked Mrs. Dunbarton to tell Mr. Lynch that I wanted to speak with him. She courteously took my name, leaned over the intercom and buzzed Mr. Lynch. I couldn't hear much of what she said but my imagination filled in the silence: "Oh, Mr. Lynch, that little faggot is here to see you."

Mr. Lynch appeared soon and, on my insistence, granted me the privacy of his office to speak to him. His office was familiar to me by now. I'd sat in it the year before when Mr. Lynch gave me that in-house suspension for cutting gym. But this time things were different.

Without mentioning Paul by name, I explained that I wanted to take a male escort to the prom. Mr. Lynch listened politely, then did exactly what I had assumed he would do.

He said no.

Mr. Lynch

I knew about the National Gay Task Force in Providence, and I decided to see if they had any advice. It took more than a week but finally I got in touch with Chuck Noice, who had tried to help Paul. Mr. Noice was too busy to get actively involved, but told me he knew someone who might be able to help.

The next day I got a phone call from John Gaffney, another member of the National Gay Task Force. He was highly enthusiastic about what I wanted to do and offered his total support. The best approach, he said, was to sue the school in federal court. The legal fees would be covered by the NGTF. This was a real stroke of luck. Like most people who want to fight for their civil rights I wouldn't have gotten far all by myself. I probably wouldn't have known any lawyers to talk to, and I certainly wouldn't have been able to pay them anything.

As if enough wasn't already happening, my mother filed for divorce that week. It was a complete surprise to me, and although it had nothing to do with my prom plans, I knew it would make the ensuing months more difficult.

A few days later I got a letter from Mr. Lynch, rationalizing his bias. He specified several reasons for having denied me my rights.

"1. The real and present threat of physical harm to you, your male escort and to others." But why did such a threat exist? It was because Mr. Lynch and others use their positions of influence to instill prejudice into others, like at the pep assembly. People aren't born with prejudice, but once they are led to believe it's right, they start to support it. Soon they discover they can feel more important if they put other people down for some reason. And finally they become principals, teachers and parents, teaching their attitudes to a whole new generation.

But Mr. Lynch wasn't about to admit his role in this vicious circle of hatred. He tried to use everyone else as the scapegoats in his second reason: "2. The adverse effect among your classmates, other students, the school and the Town of Cumberland, which is certain to follow approval of such a request for overt homosexual interaction (male or female) at a class function."

At this point I had not told Mr. Lynch that my date was to be Paul, nor had I mentioned anything about homosexuality. I had just asked permission to attend the prom with a male date. It was Mr. Lynch's own imagination that constructed visions of "overt homosexuality" taking place at the prom. I don't know exactly what he meant by it, but it's fun to guess what *he* must have been imagining. Personally I believe that "overt sexuality" of *any* kind is not proper at a prom. The heterosexual students at the prom were not doing anything that bothered other students and the Town of Cumberland, were they? Paul and I had no intention doing anything more.

Mr. Lynch's next argument was: "3. Since the dance is being

held out of state and this is a function of the students of Cumberland High School, the School Department is power-less to insure protection in Sutton, Massachusetts. That protection would be required of property as well as persons and would expose all concerned to liability for harm which might occur." But Mr. Lynch had refused to worry about protecting me when I was being physically and verbally abused right in his school; why the big fuss now? It seemed to me that he didn't care what happened to me, he was just worried about bad publicity.

His final reason was that "4. It is long standing school policy that no un-escorted student, male or female, is per-mitted to attend. To enforce this rule, a student must identify his or her escort before the committee will sell the ticket." Apparently this policy was instituted years earlier, when certain students attended the proms stag and cut in on other people's dates. It was just one of those things proving that heterosexuality is not flawless.

Mr. Lynch concluded by mentioning that I could appeal his decision to the Superintendent of Schools and the school committee, which would set up a court to hear it. Expecting them to reverse Mr. Lynch was about as sensible as expecting Siamese twins to have a duel at twenty paces. I saw no reason to appeal to the school committee.

On May first, John Gaffney arranged for me to meet with John Ward, a lawyer in Boston who handles many gay-related cases. Mr. Ward felt we could argue my case on First Amendment grounds, and he gladly agreed to represent me. We would sue Mr. Lynch personally for violating my right to equal protection under the law. I went to Mr. Lynch's office again and advised him that I was seeking a court hearing.

Also I told Mr. Lynch that I wanted to tell other students what was going on, and give them an opportunity to express their opinions. Could I appear before the student council?

No, I couldn't. Mr. Lynch said it was his fear of student violence that made him deny my request — yet hardly any students even knew what I wanted to do, much less why I wanted to do it. I knew there would be student opposition to my plans, much of it strong and irrational, but I could not believe that one hundred percent of the Cumberland student body would hate me and want to deny me my rights. At least I should get a chance to explain my decision to other students, especially if it was their potential for violence that was restricting my rights! Didn't they have a right to express their feelings on the matter before they were declared violence-prone?

But Mr. Lynch was a principal, not a civics teacher, and he didn't seem to know much about freedom of speech. He said if I wanted to speak to students as a group I could do it in my home, but not in the school. I was forbidden to discuss the situation in school with the student council. The danger of a riot was too high, he said. I couldn't believe that someone who took such a dim view of students was a high school principal.

Somehow, I wanted other students to know my plans. That way, any students who wanted to hear my viewpoint could approach me and we'd be able to talk informally. There was no way Mr. Lynch could forbid *that*. But first, students had to know.

The next day in the school library I noticed Bea Duvwalge sitting at one of the tables knitting. Bea didn't know it but she was about to be used.

"How's it going," I said to Bea, walking over and sitting down near her.

She looked at me suspiciously since we didn't exactly have a chit-chat relationship. Then I dropped the big one: "What would you say if I told you I'm attending the senior prom with Paul Guilbert as my date?"

"Gross me out to the max!" said Bea. She dropped several rows of her knitting and hurried off. By the end of the day I had told four or five other carefully-chosen gossips, and the next day most of the school knew.

Dozens of students came up and asked me if what they had heard was true. These students who approached me were the more mature ones; when I told them that yes, I was looking forward to attending the prom with Paul, none of them got hostile and some were supportive. "It's okay by me," said one kid in my science class, "But you better watch out 'cause there's kids who'll want to kill you." (For the sake of accuracy I must note that a week later, this same kid was interviewed by a newspaper reporter and said that I was ruining the prom.)

Many students who spoke to me were irritated that Mr. Lynch had predicted their reaction when he had never even consulted them. Some were worried about the publicity that a court case would generate; after the media coverage of Paul last year, people would start thinking that Cumberland was the homosexual metropolis of Rhode Island. Nobody wanted to enter their first year in college as a representative of Gaytown, U.S.A.! When people approached me with such concerns, all I could suggest was that they speak with Mr. Lynch and try to change his mind so the court case and resulting publicity would not be necessary.

Unfortunately, time for that was running out. The next day — Saturday, May tenth — I met with John Ward, John Gaffney and my new lawyer Lynette Labinger and we discussed the brief that would be filed in court that Monday. The brief said my desire to attend the senior prom with my male friend was a political and educational statement to my classmates and their escorts, to show that my dignity and value as a human being is unaffected by my sexual orientation. My lawyers confirmed my belief that I was doing something many gay men and lesbians have wanted to do in the past but weren't able to. Even though I had no doubts about what I was doing, it still felt good to hear those words of encouragement.

On Monday, May twelfth, the news broke. At seven o'clock in the morning the phone woke me up. It was a local radio station, wanting to ask some questions about my plans to go to the prom. While I was talking to them, my radio alarm clock went off and there was a call-in session on a different radio station, getting people's opinions about the prom situation in Cumberland. I picked up the newspaper; I was on the front page.

In school, the mood of the students was nothing like Mr. Lynch had anticipated. There were a few shoves in the hallway and taunts in the locker room, but I had faced all that before and had developed an obliviousness over the years. It was all old hat to me. Mr. Lynch called me into his office that morning and said he would provide protection for me if I wanted it.

I refused his offer. I knew that if there was a possibility of violence, it was because of prejudice. Protection would not put an end to prejudice: in fact, it would probably increase it. Many students who felt contempt for me also hated the school administration. If I accepted protection from the school, it would seem to some students like it was me and the administration standing against the student body. By making it clear that I was at odds with the administration, I made those students question their priorities. Who did they hate more: me, or Mr. Lynch?

Besides, Mr. Lynch's hypocrisy was repugnant to me. Where was his offer of "protection" when I had told him of the incidents in biology class? Or in gym? He didn't care about me then, because there was no danger of bad publicity, and he wouldn't have cared about me now either, if he hadn't been concerned with his public image. I felt he was offering me protection simply because it made him look good. Why should I play a part in such a sham? If he had made an announcement to the students condemning violence, I would have accepted protection.

The second day after the news broke also passed without incident. About fifty kids approached me during the day to express their support. Some showed concern, though, that media coverage would turn the prom into a spectacle.

All the students who approached me person-to-person were open to hearing what I felt. Some of them didn't like what I was doing, but they did act maturely.

On the third day, as I walked from math to environmental science class, I felt someone's hand pull back on my shoulder and a guy butted in front of me. Before I knew what was happening he had turned and punched me in the face. I fell, bleeding from a cut below my right eye.

Rapidly a group of students huddled around me. A couple of them suggested I go to the nurse, but nobody offered to help me up. Slowly regaining my composure I stood up, holding my eye, and made my way to the nurse's office. Even as I walked I was heckled by several of the students. It was a long walk. Each taunt made me more determined not to bow down, not to give in. When I finally reached the nurse's office I felt a sense of triumph. I had set my course and stuck to it, alone. Now I understood what "gay pride" really meant.

It was out of the question now to continue refusing protection. It would look like a silly attempt at heroics. Besides, this cut had required five stitches; one or two more attacks and I would be too battered up to enjoy the prom. But the attack had demonstrated to everyone the breadth and intensity of prejudice that some people feel toward any sign of another person's nonconformity.

If my attacker had been a senior, his excuse would probably have been that I was ruining "his" prom. But he wasn't. He was a junior, and wasn't even going to the prom. He obviously felt he'd be a hero to the senior class by "saving" their prom. How can I feel hostility toward someone who's misled by society to believe that heroism is synonymous with hate and violence?

This event helped put my face on the cover of all the area newspapers. People were becoming familiar with my efforts to win equal rights; it was not uncommon for someone to approach me on the street and congratulate me. As I sat in the car one day waiting for my father, a man came up to the window and said "Don't I know you from somewhere?" Then he saw the newspaper on the seat next to me, with my picture (swollen eye and all) on the front cover. He expressed his concern about my eye, and then asked me for an autograph for his children.

By that weekend, our phone was ringing constantly and my mother was getting pretty aggravated with it. There were only a few prank calls, but the reporters could be tiring too. Nobody knew where to find Paul in New York, so all their attention was focused on me.

The court hearing was set for Wednesday, May 21st, and already I was getting mail from around the eastern seaboard. One note read, "I admire what you are doing but I think you are crazy for doing it." A card from a woman who signed herself *A Compassionate Mother of Six* said that "During the struggle between you and your classmates, I offered rosaries and said many personal prayers for spiritual and physical blessings upon you and your classmates. . . ."

Court

And so, with that encouragement, and only ten days before the scheduled prom date, I entered the Federal District Courthouse in Providence with John Ward, Lynette Labinger and John Gaffney. I felt nervous knowing that I would have to testify but I had little doubt that we would win. The judge, Raymond Pettine, had a reputation for being fair and thorough and it seemed to me that the facts were on our side.

The whole student council came to the hearings, along with several other students. My friend Anne showed up and took notes. Asher and Jon promised to attend in tails and gas masks but they never made it.

Mr. Lynch gave me a tart "good morning" as I entered the courtroom. Then he reminded me that the days I was missing from school were review time for final exams. Since flunking those exams would mean spending another year at Cumberland High, I assured him that every spare minute I had would be spent studying. Then I got my best surprise. My father showed up at the court, "to give you moral support," he said. I was overjoyed.

After a brief wait, Judge Pettine entered the courtroom and the case of Fricke vs. Lynch began. There would be only two witnesses in this case: myself and Mr. Lynch. I was called to the stand.

My lawyers questioned me first. The hardest question was when they asked why I wanted to go to the prom. There were so many reasons! To give an accurate answer would have meant describing the past ten years of my life; to sum all that up in a short answer would have made me sound incoherent. So I merely explained that I felt I had the right to go to the prom like any other student. Lynette Labinger and John Ward, as my lawyers, helped me feel more at ease, and they brought out many facts that I might have overlooked.

Then Mr. Lynch's defense lawyer began questioning me.

"What is 'gay'?" he asked. I replied that it is the physical and emotional love shared by two people of the same sex and that it most certainly was something I could understand being that I had been gay since I was at least four or five.

He asked if I was bisexual. In a previous discussion with Mr. Lynch, I had said that although I was homosexual, hetero-sexuality was not beyond my realm of comprehension. Now his lawyer apparently wanted to seize on that and somehow establish that I wasn't really gay. I had told Mr. Lynch that I never went on "conventional dates" with girls, but enjoyed both female and male companionship; I do not discriminate among friends. Mr. Lynch's lawyer was now trying to inter-pret this into sexual terms. My lawyer's objection was sus-tained when I was asked how many dates I'd had with men.

Then the lawyer went off on several tangents. He asked how many times I'd been late to school and how many deten-tions I'd been given for skipping gym class. Both figures were high but seemed to me to have nothing to do with the case.

He tried to get me to say that Paul coerced me into asking him, but this was completely untrue and I said so.

He asked if I could really have fun with heterosexuals at a heterosexual dance. I told him that straight people could be comfortable without prejudice in a gay bar; why shouldn't I be comfortable at a "heterosexual" function?

He insinuated that because of my thespian interests, I was trying to become a celebrity and so further my acting career. He even questioned me about the fact that Paul had taken a girl to the soph-hop. I explained that I could not be expected to answer for Paul's actions, and the question was dropped.

The hearing got pretty informal at times. The prom was being held at the Pleasant Valley Country Club where Judge Pettine, coincidentally, often played golf. At one point he and I got into a friendly chat about his hobby; he wasn't as intimidating as I had expected a judge to be.

Some of the questions at the hearing focused on the effect my presence with Paul would have on other students at the prom. I tried to explain that while it would bother some kids, that was because they weren't used to seeing gay couples. Paul and I would just be helping them widen their range of experiences.

Besides, by no means were all the students opposed to my plans. Some were just plain indifferent to the whole thing. Others supported me wholeheartedly. Even the irrational students were changing their tune a bit. Instead of calling "faggot!" at me their taunt now was: "homosexual!"

Mr. Lynch's attorney tried to make a big deal out of the fact that Paul had worn a corsage at a gay prom held in his honor in Boston. "Are you going to wear a corsage?" he wanted to know. When he kept pushing me for an answer I said that if I chose to, I would, but at that point it had not crossed my mind.

I was still on the stand when court recessed after the first day of hearings. As I was leaving I walked over to Anne. A woman and a boy who looked about six were standing nearby. As I approached the woman grabbed the boy by the shoulders and drew him toward her. "Look," she said in a quivering voice, "that's a homosexual."

That evening I phoned Paul in New York to tell him about the day's court activities. I thought we were doing well. To my surprise, Paul was hoping the whole dance would get called off. He didn't think it was worth it any more. I told him I understood his apprehension and that I was a bit nervous myself, but that the positive aspects of our stand would transcend any threats we could possibly encounter. We talked a while longer; I assured Paul that if he really didn't want to go, he should say so. No, he said, he didn't want to disappoint me. I let it go at that.

On the second day in court, I stepped down from the witness stand after a few more questions and Mr. Lynch was sworn in. For some reason he chose sports as a major theme in his testimony. Sports were always a major concern at Cumberland High, but I was sorry to see the issue of prejudice presented as something of a giant game.

One reason he had denied my request, Mr. Lynch said, was that after Paul's prom publicity last year, our sports teams were called "faggot" and "queer" by the other teams we played. He wasn't concerned that some of these Cumberland players were the very people who had so often taunted me and Paul with the same terms. I don't like to see anybody made to feel insulted, but I couldn't find too much sympathy for the jocks in this case.

My lawyers brought in an interesting piece of evidence: the school handbook. They had Mr. Lynch read an excerpt that stated: "Prejudice, as a by-product of ignorance, is divisive and inimical to our nation's traditions."

Mr. Lynch claimed that Paul's actions the previous year had

a bad effect on students at that prom. Many kids had gotten drunk and acted like wild animals. And that had happened without an openly gay couple even present! Mr. Lynch believed that if Paul and I were actually present, things would be even worse.

Much of the excitement at that previous prom occurred when a guy ran around screaming, jumped into a lake, and showed up in his dripping wet tuxedo. He happened to be the older brother of the junior who had punched me a week earlier.

Interestingly, Mr. Lynch testified that he had often allowed two women to dance together at proms. Two women somehow didn't represent an "overt homosexual interaction"; two men did. I'm sure whole essays could be written about the attitudes behind such a thought process so I won't try to analyze it here. I just thought it was pretty goofy at the time.

When questioned, Mr. Lynch happily admitted that he had no friends who were homosexual, and that he knew little of gay lifestyles or feelings. He also testified that he disagreed with homosexual lifestyles. Yet he wanted us to believe that he did not allow his views on homosexuality to enter into his decision!

One point the defense kept making was that Mr. Lynch could not ensure protection at this prom. I found it difficult to believe he was that worried about my safety. In fact, the biggest threat to my physical well-being came when Mr. Lynch made the statement that he might cancel the prom rather than let me go with a male date. *That* statement put me in far more danger than anything else.

Finally the testimony was over. It was time for concluding statements from the lawyers. Mr. Lynch's attorney argued that our eating, dancing, and socializing at the prom would be *more* than "free speech"; it would be like yelling "Fire!" in a crowded building.

My lawyers replied that it *was* a free speech issue. My First Amendment guarantee to freedom of expression was being challenged. They also pointed out that if the case involved a black student going with a white student, no discrimination would be allowed even if some students objected violently. My case should be no different.

Judge Pettine spent a week making his decision. I heard rumors that he said it was the most difficult case he had ever heard in his fourteen years as a federal judge.

I continued studying for my finals, and life at school went on as usual. Until the court decision was announced, I think everyone's feelings were slightly in limbo. Students were asked to sell raffle tickets to help finance the prom, and I had no trouble selling my share.

The National Gay Task Force held a fund-raising party to help pay the legal fees in my case. Many people came from around Rhode Island, and the show of support was encouraging to me. Just eighteen months earlier I had been sure I would end up feeling quite lonely if were open about my homosexuality. How wrong I had been!

‛A week after we had first entered the court, Judge Pettine handed down his decision. He ruled in our favor. The First Amendment does not concern only verbal statements. The social context of an act can represent a political statement, and is therefore protected.

He pointed out that "appropriate security measures, coupled with a firm, clearly communicated attitude by the administration that any disturbance will not be tolerated, appear to be a realistic, and less restricting alternative, to prohibiting Aaron from attending the prom with the date of his choice. . . . Aaron's conduct is quiet and peaceful; it demands no response from others and in a crowd of some 500 people can be easily ignored." Any disturbance, Judge Pettine said, would clearly be the fault of those who started it, not of Paul and me. To decide otherwise would be to grant students a "hecklers' veto," allowing them to decide through prohibited and violent methods what speech will be heard. "The First Amendment," ruled Judge Pettine in his most widely-quoted statement, "does not tolerate mob rule by unruly school-children."

Judge Pettine's ruling pointed out that a different approach by Mr. Lynch might have prevented the matter from reaching the proportions it did. I think that was an especially percep-tive statement. When Mr. Lynch's lawyer had suggested that maybe I was just doing all this for publicity, he missed the fact that *I* hadn't caused the publicity. If Mr. Lynch had just let me and Paul go to the prom, there would have been only a frac-tion of the publicity that actually happened. In fact, in New Jersey that same year, a high school principal did let a gay couple go to the prom. There was hardly any media coverage of it at all. The decision also ordered Mr. Lynch to inform students that violence would not be tolerated — something he had not done previously.

Mr. Lynch and School Superintendent Condon drove up to Boston to file an appeal with the Circuit Court there. But it was thrown out immediately. We had won.

I'm sure that lots of people tried to give advice to Judge Pettine while he was preparing his ruling. I saw one letter that he got, because it came from a church pastor who knew my father. This pastor believed that my parents' breakup had caused the whole thing. "I believe this is his [Aaron's] way of asking his mother and father to come together and talk." The pastor continued with his psychoanalytical observations, noting his support for the old-fashioned family unit. "If Aaron was a real homosexual," he wrote, "and had a real conviction, then perhaps I would feel differently. . . . " He didn't even know me but he was sure he knew my innermost feelings! If I didn't want my homosexuality to be known, this man would probably have sworn that I was gay. Now that I am proud to be gay, he wants credentials. With some people you never win!

Before the Prom

The media barrage intensified after Judge Pettine's ruling came down. At my lawyers' suggestion, I held a press conference so I could state my position and squelch some of the rumors and misconceptions that were circulating. I told how proud I was that the majority of Cumberland students were dealing with the events maturely. Sure there were a few nuts, but the school should not be judged by them, I said.

On Thursday, the day before the prom, I was walking out of the school when I overheard a man in a car asking a group of students if they were seniors. They said they weren't, so I walked over and said I was a senior, what did he want?

"What do you think about this whole thing?" asked the man.

"What 'whole thing'?"

"You know, the prom issue."

"Oh," I said, "They make me sick. Homosexuals don't even belong on this earth, much less at a prom."

"Really? Then you're against what's happening?"

"*Against* it!? I'm ashamed to be a Cumberland student anymore! If homosexuals were water bugs, I'd *stomp* on them."

By this time the students in the background were in hysterics. So then the man asked, "You aren't Aaron Fricke by any chance?"

I admitted that I was. Two junior students came up to me at this point and one of them, a boy, embraced me and said "Good going, Aaron." It was one of the high points of my entire high school career.

The man introduced himself as Joe Heaney of the Boston *Herald-American* newspaper. We talked a while longer, and he wrote an excellent story.

Since Paul would not show up in time to help pick out our tuxedos, I went to the tuxedo store by myself. Many of them had already been rented; all the blacks and whites were gone, so my choice was limited. I couldn't decide what colors to get. A lavender tux was still available but I didn't want to get too tacky. Finally I phoned Paul in New York for another opinion.

"Get the lavender," said Paul. His doubts were obviously gone and he was back in form.

I said, "Right, Paul," and I took a dark navy tux for Paul and a powder blue one for myself. The school colors were blue and white and I thought this would be patriotic.

That evening, when my father took me to dinner at Smith's Restaurant in Providence, I realized that our relationship had changed. I felt close to my father in a way I had not felt for years. We still did not discuss anything sexual, of course, and he was still not perfectly comfortable with the idea that his only son was gay, but all that was overshadowed by the fact that a barrier between us had been removed. The facade I had put up to hide my homosexuality had hidden many other parts of me also. Now it was gone.

© Daniel G. Dunn/Picture Group

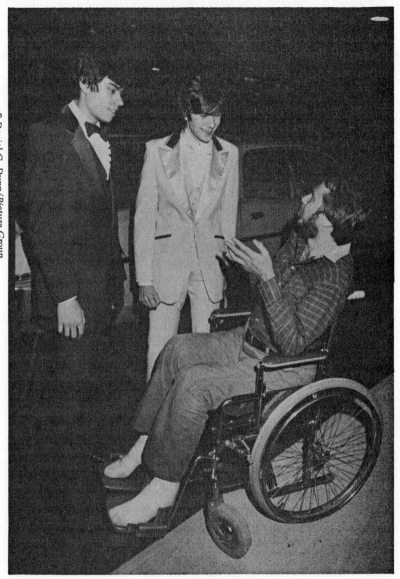

Paul and I talk with John Gaffney just before the prom.

My father said to me, "Six weeks ago I never thought I'd be sitting in a restaurant with a homosexual telling him that I loved him." Six weeks earlier he probably wouldn't have expected to hear a homosexual say the same thing back to him.

My mother found the publicity to be too much. Reporters were constantly calling, neighbors were asking her about the case, and strangers would even stop her in town and tell her their opinion on the subject. She was facing all kinds of pressures that she had never dreamed of earlier.

I guess the easiest reaction for her was to decide that I was being used by someone else, and she blamed it all on John Gaffney. She even told the newspapers that I was not responsible for my actions; John Gaffney was responsible. She was, of course, completely wrong. I still loved her, and I knew she still loved me, but it was a rough and embarrassing time for us both.

Paul's train arrived at ten o'clock Thursday evening. We were scheduled to appear on a TV program called Five All Night at two o'clock in the morning. Now that the court case was over I saw no harm in doing this one appearance with Paul. Besides, he was really excited about it.

"Five All Night" was the first of what would be quite a few talk-show appearances that Paul and I made. The host, Matt Siegel, read a press release by Roman Catholic Bishop Louis Gelineau from the Providence Archdiocese. The Bishop had condemned homosexuality and told people to stay home and pray that night. I was shocked that a man in his position would abuse his power this way. When Matt Siegel asked me what I thought of the statement I said, "Bishop Gelineau would say anything to get his name in the newspapers."

Paul spent that night at my house. My mother had not been feeling well and decided to spend time with my sister, who is a registered nurse and lives nearby, so Paul and I had the house to ourselves.

We woke up late and drove into North Providence to pick up our tuxedos, then stopped at a package store to get some wine for a little pre-prom toast. We also got a copy of the *Providence Journal-Bulletin* and found an editorial about the case: "That an individual like Aaron Fricke has a right to make a statement, with no intent to harm others, and to be accorded the same rights as his fellow students in spite of views that are unpopular, seems fundamental to our way of life and the American system."

By the time we got back to my house it was four o'clock, only three hours to go before the prom reception. We began getting the usual pre-prom jitters. John Gaffney called to say that channel six news wanted an interview. Paul was excited by the idea, but *he* hadn't been putting up with publicity day in and day out for the past month. I was fed up with it. None of the other students would be granting exclusive interviews before the prom and I didn't want to either.

We compromised. Paul went outside to give an interview, and I appeared for a quick pose with Paul, then went back in my house. I had said everything I had to say, and that was enough.

Paul and I had not danced together in over a year. We knew people would be watching us so we figured we'd better bone up. I put on my B-52's album — I loved the B-52's because of their crazy songs — and Paul and I began shoogalooing to the sharp beat and nonsense lyrics.

John Gaffney had invited us to drop by his apartment before the prom. We arrived just in time for the six o'clock news. Bishop Gelineau was on, making his pitch for heterosexuality. He also admonished students against violence: "Don't fight evil with evil" he said. I took his advice and refrained from saying what I thought of him.

It was seven o'clock by the time we had gotten into our tuxedos at John Gaffney's, dealt with the last of the reporters, and hopped into Chuck Noice's car. He had volunteered to drive us to the Pleasant Valley Country Club in Sutton, Massachusetts, where the prom was to be held.

The Prom

When we arrived at the prom site, we were greeted with a glare of television lights. Flash bulbs were popping and everybody was talking and trying to ask questions as we walked toward the building. The reporters broke down the velvet ropes that were supposed to hold them back. I was too full of anticipation and excitement to think of anything to say. So a second before walking in the door, in a grand gesture of looniness, camp and high drama, I turned to the reporters, waved, and stuck out my tongue.

Once inside, Mr. Lynch quickly ushered Paul and me away from the door, so the reporters would be unable to see us. We were shown to an empty table, which neither of us enjoyed because there were no kids to talk to. My ninth grade Spanish teacher, Mrs. Noelte, eventually sat with us.

Dinner was soon served. It was chicken cordone something or other, and consisted of mushed chicken encased in oil. My piece looked like a monster from the film *Alien*. The salad looked better but when I bit into the cherry tomato, it splattered right onto my pants. I did my best to ignore the stain but it kept showing up in the pictures people took.

After dinner was cleared away, many students began coming by to offer us a few good words. There was more good feeling than I would ever have anticipated. One after another, students came by and expresed their happiness that we could share the prom with each other. Billy Marlen came up and said he was glad to see us both. Even Dave Beamer approached and softly said, "I'm glad you're here."

Across the room, I noticed my old friend Bob Cote, accompanied by Bea Duvwalge. When Bob saw me he started to walk over, but Bea grabbed his arm and he went back to her.

I wandered over to a big picture window and stared out. Several reporters were talking outside on the lawn. For a moment I thought of all the people who would have enjoyed going to their proms with the date of their choice, but were denied that right; of all the people in the past who wanted to live respectably with the person they loved but could not; of all the men and women who had been hurt or killed because they were gay; and of the rich history of lesbians and homosexual men that had so long been ignored. Gradually we were triumphing over ignorance. One day we would be free.

The dance music came on. Kelleen Driskell came over and asked me to dance the first song with her. I was happy to accept. I'd known Kelleen in elementary school but I had drifted away from her, as from so many other people, during my fat years. We fast danced for that song and just through our physical movements together, without exchanging words, it felt as if we were re-establishing a communication.

After the dance I had to use the bathroom. Throughout the evening, Paul and I would see all kinds of defense mechanisms from the other guys whenever we went to the bathroom. Some of them made a beeline for the door as soon as we walked in. Others stayed, their desire to escape temporarily

© Daniel G. Dunn/Picture Group

Saying goodbye to Paul at the train station.

overcome by their curiosity about how gay people go to the bathroom.

When I got back to the dance floor Paul asked me if I wanted to slow dance. I did. The next song was Bob Seger's "We've Got the Night," and we stepped out onto the dance floor.

The crowd receded. As I laid my head on Paul's shoulder I saw a few students start to stare at us. I closed my eyes and listened to the music, my thoughts wandering over the events of that evening. When the song ended, I opened my eyes. A large crowd of students had formed a ring around us. Probably most of them had never before seen two happy men embracing in a slow dance. For a moment I was uncomfortable. Then I heard the sound that I knew so well as a B-52's fan. One of my favorite songs was coming up: "Rock Lobster."

Paul and I began dancing freestyle. Everyone else was still staring at us, but by the end of the first stanza, several couples had also begun dancing. The song has a contagious enthusiasm to it, and with each bar, more dancers came onto the floor.

I glanced over at the tables. Bob Cote was sitting with Bea Duvwalge, who was finishing off her chicken cordone-whatever. Bob was eyeing the dancing students and bouncing his leg with an obvious urge to join. He stood up and tugged at Bea's arm to come with him; she pulled him back and he sat down again with a look of disappointment.

More students were coming onto the floor to dance. I doubt that any two people were dancing with the same movements: the dancing was an expression of our individuality, and no one felt bad about being different. Everyone was free to be themselves.

A quarter of the way into the song, thirty people were on the dance floor. I looked at Bob and Bea again. Bea seemed to be wondering what a rock lobster was.

"Down, Down, Down," commanded the lyrics. Everyone

on the dance floor sank to their knees and crouched on the ground. I lifted my head slightly to look around. Dozens of intertwining bodies crouched on their knees as if praying. We were all one; we shared a unity of pure love. And those who did not want to share it, such as Bea Duvwalge, sat on the sidelines. Bea was now arguing with Bob.

Red snappers snappin'
Clamshells clappin'

Everyone jumped to their feet again and resumed dancing. Many more kids had joined us and there must have been sixty or eighty people on the dance floor now.

As Paul and I danced, we had gradually drifted from our original space on the floor. We were now near the table where Bob and Bea sat. Out of the corner of my eye I saw Bea suddenly stand up and grab a napkin. It looked like a glass of water had spilled on her. She dabbed at her gown.

"Down, Down, Down" cried the B-52's again, and we all went down. The feeling of unity among us permeated the air again. When we came up I heard Bea yelling at Bob, then she stormed off toward the bathroom. Now there were at least a hundred people on the dance floor. The tempo became more frenetic and everyone danced faster.

"Let's Rock!!!" bellowed from the speakers, and to my surprise, when I looked up I saw that Paul had disappeared. In his place was Bob Cote. I looked around; several other guys were dancing with each other, and girls were dancing with girls. Everybody was rockin', everybody was fruggin'. Who cared why? Maybe they were doing it to mock me and Paul, maybe they were doing it because they wanted to, maybe one was an excuse for the other. . . I didn't know and I didn't care. It was fun. Everyone was together. Eventually Bob and I drifted away. I danced with girls, I danced with guys, I danced with the entire group.

Then the music stopped. "Rock Lobster" has an abrupt

ending, and no one was quite ready for it to stop. I had been having so much fun that I lost track of time; I had also lost track of Paul, and had to look around the room for him.

I could see that everyone felt a sense of disorientation. For six minutes and forty-nine seconds, the students on the dance floor had forgotten about their defenses, forgotten about their shells. We just had fun.

After the Prom

We were invited to my friend Cindy Hannah's house after the prom, but I had forgotten to ask for her address. So Paul and I stopped briefly at the Fife and Drum, a gay bar in Providence. Then I headed back to Cumberland to get some sleep.

Monday was the only school day left before graduation. It was the day for getting exam grades and final report cards. Several kids commented to me about how much fun they had at the prom, and that everybody's worries had been unnecessary. My friend Kathy came up to me and said, "Hey, Aaron, I loved that new wave dance."

An hour before graduation I stopped in the school office to pick up my yearbook. I walked into Mr. Lynch's office to thank him for the protection he had given me. In a very serious tone of voice he said, "You know, Aaron, if this question ever arises again, my answer to other homosexuals will be the same." This must have been his way of trying to get the last laugh. Now that I was leaving, he could again run his school in the stifling manner he wanted. I seethed inside, but I said nothing. I had made my statement already.

For the commencement exercises, I was escorted to the football field by Mr. DeGoes. He asked why I was wearing a pink triangle on my gown. I explained that the Nazis had persecuted homosexuals as well as Jews, and had forced gay concentration camp prisoners to wear a pink triangle for identification. I wore it in honor of all the gay people who had suffered from oppression and prejudice. It was the least I could do in their honor. "Oh," said Mr. DeGoes. .

As other students went to their seats, several of them made comments when they passed me. A few were derogatory. Then, a small, very pretty girl called me, looked me in the eye and said, "I love you." She walked by so quickly that I lost sight of her in the crowd. I didn't know her name. But that voice was so familiar. Then it dawned on me: it was the voice I had so often heard on the phone when I was most lonely and in need of communication. It was the clicker. I looked for her but she was gone.

I took my place with the graduating class. I was happy at last to feel like every other student, with nobody standing around me as protection. The band played "Pomp and Circumstance" as we marched onto the football field. The bleachers overflowed with friends and relatives of the graduating seniors.

It was speech time. Mr. Lynch made a few predictable Lynch-type comments, then to my surpise he chastized some seniors who had been caught the night before painting FAGGOT CITY on the school. They would not be allowed to participate in graduation. Mr. Condon, the school superintendent, spoke of preserving American values in the tradition of Abraham Lincoln and Harry Truman. But his actions that spring had not been very reminiscent of Abraham Lincoln!

The valedictorian gave a rousing speech on individuality.

Then, the names of graduating seniors were called, and one by one they approached the podium. When my name was called, I apprehensively stood up and walked forward. A swell of boos and cackles rose from the bleachers. My stomach tightened. I had not expected the reaction to be this bad! Then I realized that within this hostile cacophony there was a fainter sound, a sound of cheers and applause coming from another direction. Among the graduating class, many seniors were cheering for me. I turned to them and took a deep bow to show my love and respect.

Afterword

In this book I have talked about many unpleasant experiences but I do not blame my torments on heterosexuality. I have been friends with many loving, open-minded heterosexuals. The thing I blame has no sexuality. It is the nameless, faceless entity of prejudice and oppression. Often that oppression has taken a physical form in people who are straight; perhaps those people are themselves just pawns, trapped in a vicious cycle of oppression. I am only reporting their actions as I have experienced them.

The prom case brought about many good changes. It exposed people to the gay rights issue. It encouraged them to look at it more rationally than they might have otherwise. The hatred that many people feel when they hear the word "gay" must have diminished after the fourteenth time they heard it on the six o'clock news.

The media often handled this case well. The day Judge Pettine's ruling was announced, reporter Bob Blanchard came on the news and said:

"Those who support equal rights for gay people say today's decision is a major victory.... In reality, however, it was not.... because the much larger question of rampant discrimination gay people face in housing and the job market remains."

Although the prom case is a bit more serious than the Village People's song "YMCA," its main value was to bring the issue to the attention of the public and make them aware that there *is* a problem, a problem that remains to be solved.

Parents sometimes teach their children that homosexuality is a disease whereas homophobia is not. Actually, it is the contrary. Homophobia is a degeneration of respect for other humans and it is contagious. One person exhibits hatred toward a gay person, impressionable people see it, and they recreate those actions. Parents who teach their children to hate or fear homosexuals do not realize that *their* children could be homosexuals. Prejudiced attitudes serve only to confuse the children, whether they have homosexual tendencies or not.

My last day at Cumberland High School ended on a particularly sad note. As I walked off the football field after commencement, now escorted by several uniformed policemen, two children approached me before I stepped into my car. "Faggot!" one said. "You queer," said the other. I had never felt so defenseless. They were only about ten years old and I felt no hostility toward them. But I pity the society that sits back and encourages children to feel bitterness and hatred toward anything.

I live with pride every day of my life now. Pride in the idea that my openness can set an example for all people about the benefits of being open. My memories of the oppression I felt will not be forgotten, nor will my awareness that people continue to experience these emotional deprivations. But I am now confident that I *can* overcome the barriers that hetero-sexual prejudice will present.

Even so, I will be reminded *daily* of the torments gay people face. My writing will hopefully serve as a vehicle to make others more actively aware. I will remind heterosexuals that we are human. And I will remind gay people struggling for a positive identity that, in the words of André Gide: "It is better to be hated for what one is than loved for what one is not."

Epilog

During the summer Paul and I appeared on several talk shows, including Phil Donahue. A number of people, many of them teenagers, wrote to us afterwards; here's what some of them said.

୧୭

. . . I want to thank you for going to your prom and for appearing on the Donahue show. I am the mother of a gay son who is now age 20. He didn't go to any of his high school proms because at that time in his life he wasn't free to be himself. It was a very hard time.

It is time we let people know that young gays are needlessly shut out and discriminated against. Your appearance should help to increase this understanding. . . .

D.H. (Gulf Way, Florida)

୧୭

. . . I read about you in *People* magazine and I feel you had a right to take the date of your choice to your high school prom. There are many males in this world who are like you, including me. But that does not mean it is right. I want to change and I know I can change. We all know being gay is wrong. It will make people uncomfortable when they see you and your male friend.

I hope this does not hurt your feelings. I just wanted to let you know that you can change if you want to. I am going to change.

Stanley (Durham, North Carolina)

 è•

I am 16 years old. I don't date, because I don't know if I am gay or not. Just the thought of intercourse with a boy makes me ill. (I have a strong stomach.) If my mother knew I was writing to you she'd be furious. But then she always says what a person does in their bedroom is their business. I wish you and Paul all the best luck in your future.

Patti (Jackson, Minnesota)

è•

I am a 16 year old high school girl and I wish more kids had the courage to do what you did. I think it's a shame that society has programmed us into believing that being gay is something to be ashamed of. I am heterosexual and have a boyfriend and am very happy. I think everyone has a right to be as happy as me, no matter what their sexuality.

Libby (Houston, Texas)

è•

...I am in high school myself, going into my senior year, and have become increasingly aware of certain bisexual, if not altogether lesbian, feelings. I was faced with a similar situation at my prom. Fortunately I go to a small (fifty students) school, and was responsible for organizing the prom, so nobody paid too much attention to who went with who. I went with a girlfriend of mine and two male friends and had a fair time.

I think homosexuality is a beautiful and honest form of self-expression. The way I see it, if you are comfortable with your own body then you will know the other person's body doubly well; the experience can only be total nirvana. I say that because I have not, as of yet, had a lesbian experience. I suppose the reason is that I have been brought up with a lot of guilt by very conservative parents. The mothers of both the girl I babysit for and my once-best friend are both lesbians and my mother knows it. She doesn't like them and we are more and more at odds with each other.

I have yet to discover a friend I can be truly honest with, as you did with Paul. But when I do I am sure it will be wonderful.

Linda (Harrisburg, Pennsylvania)

ॐ

I saw you on Donahue today! Boy I am sure glad that you fags are back there and not out here in Phoenix! The way the both of you talked really proved that you were as "faggy as a baggy"! Very frankly if it were my high school I would not of gone near the prom! Just like when a black moves into a white neighborhood all the white people move out! It's the same way with you faggy baggies! You are so special! The only good thing about gay peple is that they can't have kids, and I am sure glad of about that!

Fags are queer!!! Stay back there in Boston!!!!!

The Mushroom (Phoenix, Arizona)

ॐ

...I am very proud of you for being so open. For me just being gay is tough enough without being public about it. I have permitted myself to be gay for the last nine or ten months and have enjoyed having my feelings very much. But I continue to lead a straight life. My girlfriends, my friends and my family all believe I am the All-American Boy who will have three kids, a dog and a 20-year mortgage.

My conscience doesn't bother me because I too am proud to be gay. It's made me happier than all those straight years put together.

John (Lawton, Oklahoma)

ॐ

...I have been "out of the closet" for six months now and feel absolutely wonderful. My mother is very supportive of me. She has known since last December and there was no shock at all. I have since found out that she is also gay!

Now everyone that I love knows about me. The reactions have

been on the whole very pleasant. My girl friends treat me very much the same, but my male friends seem to shy away a bit. But who cares? They can accept me like I am or they can go get lost.

It seems to me that as soon as I put out the energy of being gay, a lot of my friends have turned out to be gay....

Steve (Salinas, California)

ૐ

I'm so glad I saw you on the Phil Donahue show. It was a relief and an encouragement for me. I'm 18, recently graduated from high school, and (at this time) gay. I was never open with my feelings until about a year ago when I told some close friends and family. My friends are very supportive and helpful — my mother and father try to be supportive, but I know it is very hard for them to deal with. It is hard for me to deal with also, but talking with friends, and generally opening myself up to my real feelings, help a lot.

I do not (to my knowledge) have any gay friends and since I am not attracted to the disco scene it is not easy to meet other people who are gay. But I'm not giving up hope, because I know that there are lots of gay people all over....

Realizing you're gay (to me) is like being born; there is so much to do — much internal growth and strengthening is needed, as well as outward action in order to be free to be what you are. There is also the element of doubt which can be very disturbing. When I look into a mirror, I see myself — what I look like physically. If I were black, I would see myself as such, and thus could be distinguished as a minority by way of the senses. But you can't see what gay is, it's just what a person is....

Bob (Beaverton, Oregon)

ૐ

Hi! My name is Mark and I live in a small community in east Tennessee. And like you, I'm gay. My family is very religious and everybody in our community knows each other so I don't know if I will ever "come out." But I'm not saying I haven't had a gay sexual experience. I have. As a matter of fact it was with the pastor's son, Joey. Until I met him I wasn't sure I was gay but when I met him it was true love.

Joe isn't gay. He says that he is bisexual but only with me. Does that make sense? Do you think a guy can be bisexual with just one guy and heterosexual with everyone else? I haven't told him that I am gay. I have confided everything to him but that. If I tell him I'm gay I'm afraid it will hurt our relationship and I couldn't stand that.

Mark

ट๑

. . . I'm really glad that you could be public about being gay. I can't see why people should get so upset. But I remember when I was little, in Sunday School, there was a Bible verse saying it was wrong to be gay. It's so confusing!

I know a lot of gay people. I'm not gay because of how my family would feel if I was. My brother *hates* gays. And he has threatened one of my gay friends. . . .

I don't think I'll ever be gay, but if I do I don't think it's wrong. I just turned 18 and love very much being a girl and going out with guys, but they do get to be a drag. Some of them are such assholes, excuse me, but that's all the credit I can give them. . . .

Katie (San Mateo, California)

ट๑

First of all I want to congratulate you. You opened a new door for the gay people of the United States. I just wish I could be so brave.

I'm nearly 17 now and still have not told my parents although, like you, most of the kids at my high school know that I am gay. Few give me a hard time; it's getting better.

I really don't know how my parents would react if I told them. They probably wouldn't be too surprised. I'm sure my parents and all four of my sisters are wise to me. Being homosexual is kind of hard to hide, don't you agree? Could you give me some tips on how to go about telling them? Or should I tell them at all?

Joseph (San Antonio, Texas)

ट๑

. . . I'm 18 and for the past four years I have known I was bisexual. It is very hard for me. I would like nothing more than to come out. But I don't think I could handle that much pressure. I guess I'm afraid of what my family and friends would say — especially the ones that I've known for many years. I get uptight about going to clubs or anything and I find it extremely difficult to meet other gay people, especially my age.

I wish there were some open people, like you, in my high school. I would like to have known you two, just to talk to. Lots of times I'd like to just talk to someone who understands. . . .

To tell you the truth just writing you makes me feel better. I feel I opened up, even if its just a little.

Eric (North Miami Beach, Florida)

ଈ

I saw you on TV and want to say: GOOD FOR YOU AND PAUL! This is my husband's opinion also. We applaud you for standing on your ground and doing what you thought was best. I wish more people could be as open!

I became aware of homosexuals in my teens and my mom taught me to believe everyone is equal regardless of color, creed or beliefs, and I carry that thought today!

Mr. and Mrs. R.H. (Reno, Nevada)

ଈ

Bravo! You did exactly what my girlfriend and I want to do but probably will not. But it was encouraging to see someone else be so brave. And who knows, maybe Annie and I *will* be that brave in time for next year's prom!

June (Denver, Colorado)

Also available from
Alyson Publications

☐ **ONE TEENAGER IN TEN,** edited by Ann Heron, $4.00. One teenager in ten is gay. Here, twenty-six young people from around the country discuss their experiences: coming out to themselves, to parents, and friends; trying to pass as straight; running away; incest; trouble with the law; making initial contacts with the gay community; religious concerns; and more. Their words will provide encouragement for other teenagers facing similar experiences.

☐ **ALL-AMERICAN BOYS,** by Frank Mosca, $6.00. "I've known I was gay since I was thirteen. Does that surprise you? It didn't me. Actually, it was the most natural thing in the world. I thought everyone was. At least until I hit high school. That's when I finally realized all those faggot and dyke stories referred to people like me...." So begins this story of a teenage love affair that should have been simple — but wasn't.

☐ **CRUSH,** by Jane Futcher, $8.00. It wasn't easy fitting in at an exclusive girls' school like Huntington Hill. But in her senior year, Jinx finally felt as if she belonged. Lexie — beautiful, popular Lexie — wanted her for a friend. Jinx knew she had a big crush on Lexie, and she knew she had to do something to make it go away. But Lexie had other plans. And Lexie always got her way.

☐ **THE GAY BOOK OF LISTS,** by Leigh Rutledge, $8.00. Rutledge has compiled a fascinating and informative collection of lists. His subject matter ranges from history (6 gay popes) to politics (9 perfectly disgusting reactions to AIDS) to entertainment (12 examples of gays on network television) to humor (9 Victorian "cures" for masturbation). Learning about gay culture and history has never been so much fun.

☐ **BETWEEN FRIENDS,** by Gillian E. Hanscombe, $8.00. The four women in this book represent radically different political outlooks and sexualities, yet they are tied together by the bonds of friendship. Through their experiences, recorded in a series of letters, Hanscombe deftly portrays the close relationship between political beliefs and everyday lives.

☐ **COMING OUT RIGHT,** by Wes Muchmore and William Hanson, $8.00. Every gay man can recall the first time he stepped into a gay bar. That difficult step often represents the transition from a life of secrecy and isolation into a world of unknowns. The transition will be easier for men who have this recently updated book. Here, many facets of gay life are spelled out for the newcomer, including: coming out at work; gay health and the AIDS crisis; and the unique problems faced by men who are coming out when they're under 18 or over 30.

☐ **IN THE TENT,** by David Rees, $7.00. Seventeen-year-old Tim is sensitive, intellectual, and gay. His homosexuality is a source of increasing conflict for him, especially when he becomes aware of his attraction to his straight friend Aaron. Then, on a camping trip with two other boys, Tim and Aaron are forced to deal with the issues they've so carefully avoided.

☐ **CHOICES,** by Nancy Toder, $8.00. Lesbian love can bring joy and passion; it can also bring conflicts. In this straightforward, sensitive novel, Nancy Toder conveys the fear and confusion of a woman coming to terms with her sexual and emotional attraction to other women.

☐ **BETTER ANGEL,** by Richard Meeker, $7.00. The touching story of a young man's gay awakening in the years between the World Wars. Kurt Gray is a shy, bookish boy growing up in a small town in Michigan. Even at the age of thirteen he knows that somehow he is different. Gradually he recognizes his desire for a man's companionship and love. As a talented composer, breaking into New York's musical world, he finds the love he's sought.

☐ **THE TWO OF US,** by Larry J. Uhrig, $7.00. Any two people trying to build a fulfilling relationship today face some major hurdles. A gay or lesbian couple faces even more potential problems. Here, Larry Uhrig, pastor of the Metropolitan Community Church in Washington, D.C., draws on his experience counseling gay couples to provide a practical handbook about how to make a gay relationship work.

☐ **IN THE LIFE,** edited by Joseph Beam, $9.00. When writer and activist Joseph Beam became frustrated that so little gay literature spoke to him as a black gay man, he did something about it: the result was *In the Life,* an anthology which takes its name from a black slang expression for "gay." Here, thirty-three writers and artists explore what it means to be doubly different — black and gay — in modern America. Their stories, essays, poetry, and artwork voice the concerns and aspirations of an often silent minority.

☐ **THE ALYSON ALMANAC,** by Alyson Publications staff, $9.00. Almanacs have been popular sources of information since "Poor Richard" first put his thoughts on paper and Yankee farmers started forecasting the weather. Here is an almanac for gay and lesbian readers that follows these traditions. You'll find the voting records of members of Congress on gay issues, practical tips on financial planning for same-sex couples, an outline of the five stages of a gay relationship, and much, much more.

☐ **UNNATURAL QUOTATIONS,** by Leigh W. Rutledge, $9.00. The author of *The Gay Book of Lists* has put together an entertaining collection of quotations by, for, or about gay men and lesbians. Hundreds of figures — both past and present, homophilic and homophobic — are represented here. Well illustrated and indexed for handy reference, *Unnatural Quotations* promises the same excitement generated by *The Gay Book of Lists.*

Albuquerque Academy Library
6400 Wyoming Blvd. NE
Albuquerque, NM 87109

Ask for these titles in your favorite bookstore. Or, to order by mail, use this coupon or a photocopy.

Enclosed is $_____$ for the following books. (Add $1.00 postage when ordering just one book. If you order two or more, we'll pay the postage.)

1. _____

2. _____

3. _____

4. _____

name: _____

address: _____

city: _____ state: _____ zip: _____

ALYSON PUBLICATIONS
Dept. B-09, 40 Plympton St., Boston, MA 02118

After June 30, 1992, please write for current catalog.